TOTALLY TUNELESS
An Alphabetical Anthology of Almost Every Song Lyric
1984 - 2014

by
MITCH FRIEDMAN

Cover design by Mitch Friedman
Album cover designs by Mitch Friedman,
Anne D. Bernstein, and The Design Studio
Author photograph by Doug Miller
Printed by CreateSpace

Published by Lewis Avenue Books
lewisavenuebooks@gmail.com

All lyrics ©1987, 1988, 1990, 1999,
2002, 2005, 2008, 2013, 2014
by Mitch Friedman

Totally Tuneless Copyright © 2014 Mitch Friedman
All rights reserved.
ISBN: 0986300837
ISBN-13: 978-0-9863008-3-7

Table of Contents

	Discography	vii
1	A Life In a Day	1
2	A Lost Clown	3
3	A Million Feet Tall	5
4	Abigail	7
5	All The Best To You and Yours	8
6	As Moons Go	9
7	Assassinational	10
8	At The Broken Heart Shop	11
9	Bad Magician	13
10	Bad Vibes	14
11	Blackout	15
12	Blues In My Beer	16
13	Boan-Ga-Loar	17
14	Brother Nature	18
15	Can't Spend a Cent	19
16	Car Rap	20
17	Chants of Rain	21
18	Clickin' and Surfin'	22
19	Color Feel	23
20	Comfort Zone	24
21	Contagious	26
22	Crack The Case	28
23	Dear So & So	29
24	Dinner For None	30
25	Do The Milkshake	31
26	Do-Re-Mimi	32
27	Don't Get The Gods Mad	33
28	Don't Hold a Grudge	35
29	Everything Makes Me Cry	37
30	Fairy Tale	38
31	Flavor Day	39
32	From Soup To Nuts	40
33	Gibberish	42
34	Halfway to Heaven	43
35	Hazy Recollection	44
36	Hope-Rope It!	45

37	I Hate Love	46
38	I Have Never Lied	48
39	I Hope	50
40	I Miss My Daddy	51
41	I Need a Hug	52
42	I See You	53
43	I Wish I Was a Kid Again	54
44	I'm Gonna Rock My Baby Tonight	57
45	Ice Me Nice	58
46	If Every Day Was Christmas	59
47	In The Know	60
48	Indian Giver	62
49	Indoor Wildlife	64
50	Invisibility	65
51	Is Love There?	66
52	It Won't Be Long Now	67
53	Keep It a Secret	69
54	Kloreen	70
55	La Bomba	71
56	Laura	72
57	Let Me Be Your Pet	75
58	Little Masterpiece	76
59	Make It Snappy	78
60	Make Yourself at Home	80
61	Mesmerized	81
62	Mr. Sir	82
63	My Dumb Luck	84
64	My Second Record	86
65	Neon Moon	87
66	New Kind of Human	88
67	New York Sunset	90
68	Nine Mile Road	92
69	Nothing But a Soul	93
70	Often I Saunter	95
71	Once	96
72	One Billion Degrees Below	97
73	One Side at a Time	99
74	Open	100
75	Out of It	102

76	Pip Squeak	104
77	Pluto	105
78	President	106
79	Pretty Pretty New York City	108
80	Previously Unreleased	110
81	Purple Burt	112
82	Reach By Speech	113
83	Ribbons & Bows	114
84	Runaway Train of Thought	115
85	She Was Sooooooooooooo Hot!	116
86	She's Dynamite!	117
87	Shedding One's Tread	118
88	Simplification	119
89	Sing Anyway	121
90	666-Luck	122
91	Sleepless	123
92	Sleeptown	124
93	Slow Down Now	126
94	Smile Awhile	128
95	Splendid	130
96	Spring (Is Waiting For a Chance To) Spring	131
97	Steal This	132
98	Summer Morning, I'm Due	133
99	Superstar Maker To The Stars	134
100	Swingin'	136
101	Swinging On The Family Tree	138
102	The Last Nice Day	140
103	The Man That Talked Too Much	141
104	The Mitch & Jude Show	143
105	The Pageant Song	144
106	The Popcorn Tree	146
107	This Fitting Room	147
108	This Friend	148
109	This Is a Song	149
110	Thrash Dash	151
111	To Be There For You	152
112	Today Night	154
113	Treasure	155
114	Tribute Band	156

115	Trick-Knee Trixie	158
116	Truth Decay	159
117	Try This On For Size	160
118	What a Gas!	162
119	What Goes Around Comes Around	164
120	When I Was Your Age	165
121	When Your Number's Up	167
122	Where'd Ya Get That Dirt?	169
123	Who May I Say Is Calling?	170
124	Wonder Where	172
	About the Author	174

Discography

I started writing lyrics in the summer of 1984, and have continued to this day. Most ended up in recorded songs, but several are still waiting patiently for some musical matchmaking.

pOp cOrn (1987) --- 90-minute audiocassette album containing *When I Was Your Age: A nostalgic look at the present* (1984 - 1985), *Excuse Me* (1985 - 1987), and *Scrap* (1984-87)

EXTRAVAGANZA DELUXE! (1988) --- 45-minute audiocassette album

HENWAY - Big Hair (1990) --- 60-minute audiocassette album

The Importance of Sauce (1999) --- CD

FRED (2002) --- CD

Purple Burt (2005) --- CD

Game Show Teeth (2008) --- CD

SING SING (2013) --- CD

For CDs and digital downloads, visit
bandcamp.com
cdbaby.com
amazon.com
itunes

A Life In a Day

Woke up, got out of bed
fried a dryer 'cross my head
My doctor said I have a day to live
and I'd better get started because this is it
"Will I last the night?" I asked the doc
"Depends on how you set your clock"

Four hemispheres, seven continents
Four billion people and I owe my rent
Got a lot to do and one hour's spent
Twenty-three to go, thirty years that went

Sprint with a glint and a smile in my eye
Hi, how are you? Hi, how are you?
Shook the hand of each man and child
Hi, how are you? Hi, how are you?

Had a one-second date with one thousand women
Be my bride, be my bride
Flirted with the rest 'til my heart was swimming
Not tonight, not tonight

Was a monk, was a junkie
Swung from trees like a monkey
Moussed my hair into punky
Pinned a tail on a donkey

Drove a car, flew a plane
Sped a boat in the rain
Picked some cotton and cane
Trained a wild Great Dane

Sampled every food like a smorgasbord
What I couldn't finish I sure did hoard
and dropped it on all the hungry people
Paid my respects at each church and steeple

Read a page in every book
Found the ones in progress and snuck a look
Viewed every photo ever took
Checked out a cranny and a nook

Delivered twenty babies simultaneously
Killed lots of criminals heinously
Cured cancer, AIDS, and the common cold
Found a way to keep bread free of mold
Hosted auctions until all art was sold
Mined all of the remaining gold

Well I did all I could that I thought was best
Even trounced every single insect pest
While I took a one-millisecond rest
I died prematurely from cardiac arrest
Even God had six days
and was probably stressed
If he could see me now he'd be impressed

The doctor's news turned out as good
'cause I did everything that I ever would

(unrecorded)

A Lost Clown

I slowly shuffle along the street
Red oversized shoes on my feet
Caked facial makeup streaks from the heat
My baggy polka-dotted pants
are sagging 'cause they're soiled

All kinds of circus freaks pass me by
and enter buildings that scrape the sky
They're really not that different than I,
except they have a place to eat and sleep
which makes them spoiled

I'm a lost clown
Can somebody help me?
Somebody help me to find my way around
I'll wear a frown until somebody tells me
where to find the children
who will laugh at me in this town

I juggle soda cans for a dime
or even do some tired, old mime
Most anything to pass the time
until Mr. Ringling
and his brothers come to find me

My head still hurts from when I was mugged
by a pack of screaming thugs who were drugged
They crushed my pompom hat and I'm bugged
but I've got my bloodied bow tie
and bent horn just to remind me

I'm a lost clown
Can somebody help me?
Somebody help me to find my way around
I'll wear a frown until somebody tells me
where to find the children
who will laugh at me in this town

A city sidewalk isn't where to do a pratfall
unless your curly wig
can help you tune out catcalls
This is one unfriendly big top
The ringleaders all dress as cops
Trapeze accidents happen all day

I am devoted to entertain
A day without applause causes pain,
but no one claps on a subway train
Why are people so afraid to express enjoyment?

Birthday parties are everywhere. . .
The sights and sounds of a country fair. . .
These memories are too much to bear
for a circus type whose biggest gripe
is hopeless unemployment

I'm a lost clown
Can somebody help me?
Somebody help me to find my way around
I'll wear a frown until somebody tells me
where to find the children
who will laugh at me in this town

(from *The Importance of Sauce*)

A Million Feet Tall

I'm a million feet tall
(He's a million feet tall)

I'm doing a jig
but I am so big
they can feel my moves in the next port of call

My two-step is wide
and a Cuban slide
would glide the whole length of America's Mall

I'm a million feet tall
(He's a million feet tall)

When doing a waltz
the air traffic halts
In fact I can't get down unless I crawl

I'm trying to dance
but sneaking a glance
I don't domino most of the Great Wall

I'm a million feet tall
(He's a million feet tall)

I never have leapt
and my one quick step
is the equivalent of one trillion of y'all

I once did ballet
way back in the day
Every pirouette increased the urban sprawl

I'm a million feet tall
(He's a million feet tall)

I could boogaloo
but if I were you,
jump on the next jet and head up to Nepal

If I did a tap
get all set to clap
A tsunami will precede my curtain call

I got legs and I know how to use them

You better watch my step

189.39393939 miles high

Look out, look out below

I'm movin' on up

(unrecorded)

Abigail

I am the coffin and she is the nail
She is the anthrax and I am the mail
I am the blindness and she is the braille
She is the epic and I am the fail

I shudder when I need her touch
This 1 + 1 is 1 too much
Abigail

No pain, no gain
She's the bane of my existence
Major problems seem so minor
squinting at them from a distance

She is the bloodhound and I am the trail
She is the heavy and I am the scale
I am the handcuff and she is the jail
She is the Ahab and I am the whale

I shiver if I need her touch
This 1 + 1 is 1 too much
Abigail

(from *SING SING*)

All The Best To You and Yours

As klieg lights sweep across the starry sky,
heaven knows it must be time to say goodbye
Tiny teardrops rinse the twinkle from my eyes
So before you head for the exit door
I wish you

All the best to you and yours

(from *The Importance of Sauce*)

As Moons Go

There's nothing for sure
so perfectly pure
or has more allure than a kiss
With lust in my eyes
you deem it unwise
At least please indulge me in this?

As moons go,
this one is luminous and bright
As moons go,
the sun is swooning through the night
Romance may wane
but chance remains
this night so glorious for us, as moons go

With such universal appeal
your pull on my heart strings is real
A relationship, can I land it?
Without you I shan't even plan it

No dream can eclipse
the gleam of your lips
after we shared sips of champagne
My countdown fell short
on your mission abort
Is it lunacy to still proclaim . . .?

As moons go,
that one was luminous and bright
As moons go,
the sun was crooning through the night
Poetic I wax
but let's face the facts
That night was glorious for us, as moons go

(from *Game Show Teeth*)

Assassinational

Up until now,
assassination has been TOP SECRET BUSINESS
But with the new Assassinational credit card,
being an accomplice to murder
is only a phone call away!

Need some killing done? We'll take credit for it
ASSASSINATIONAL
We issue a monthly statement

Presidents
Heads of state
Figure heads
You dictate
where and when,
who you hate
Then we eliminate

Car bombs
Letter bombs
Let us bomb their hotel
You select the type of kill,
we guarantee to do it well

Poison snakes
Poison drinks
Dripping water on the head
ASSASSINATIONAL
We'll insure that they are dead

(from *pOp cOrn*)

At The Broken Heart Shop

"Good morning. I'm sorry. How can I help you?"
questioned the man who stood at the counter
"My woman has left me. She took little bits of my ticker.
I think I need a repair."
"It's worse than you thought. You're missing a chamber.
Here is loaner, come back in three days."
The customer smiled, though rather meekly,
whispered a "Thank you" and skulked out the door
At the Broken Heart Shop

"Good morning. I'm sorry. How can I help you?"
questioned the man who stood at the counter
"The unit you loaned me suffered a rupture
after a beautiful girl said hello."
"Your timing is perfect. The chamber you needed
has been replaced. Pay me $10.98."
The customer exchanged the money and organs
and gingerly tiptoed out the red door
At the Broken Heart Shop

"Good morning. I'm sorry. How can I help you?"
questioned the worker, a bit annoyed
"I've been unlucky for the third time.
I saw a sad movie. It split into slivers."
"You'll need a whole new one. I've done all I can for you.
I would suggest that you never leave home."
The customer whimpered, acknowledged the advice
and defeatedly walked to the street
At the Broken Heart Shop

"Some folks have no luck"
the customer thought
"All of this love stuff could be for naught"

The customer came back, just three days later,
to return his one heart
He had given up

But behind the counter there now stood a lady -
Angelic, voluptuous, available
"How can I help you?" asked the new woman
"I think I love you. Can I share your heart?"
They signed an agreement and agreed to meet
the next evening, shortly past closing time
At the Broken Heart Shop

The following morning the man was awakened
by a tremendously loud and sweet sound
He thought he was dreaming, but much to his horror
the Happiness Hydrogen Bomb had been dropped
All living creatures, forever and ever
would now be ecstatic and filled up with love
He ran at his fastest to meet his new woman
The sign on the door said "CLOSED FOR GOOD"
At the Broken Heart Shop

(from *The Importance of Sauce*)

Bad Magician

Magical illusion, tragical conclusion
No one knows just how it's done
and no one really cares

With a bad magician,
mirrors don't even enter the picture

(from *pOp cOrn*)

Bad Vibes

They take a midnight drive, goin' 95,
to a seedy dive where the low-lifes thrive
just to imbibe 'till their brains get fried
Then they dance/collide
Lookin' beady-eyed, they speak of bribe,
then threaten lives playin' games with knives
And if you can't confide or you're speakin' snide
they'll get evil-eyed like Bonnie and Clyde,
so you'd better hide or . . . homicide
Ooooooooh,
Bad vibes

When a member of some cult or tribe,
whose dislike is wide
'cause they dress drip-dried as they abuse wives
strides to your side and talks contrived,
trying to deride with vile lies and diatribe
just to kill your pride
Which your nice inside could just let slide
But you get tongue-tied, wanna skin their hide
with your ugly side
and instead you cry, cry, cry
If something doesn't jive with this change of tide
I have just described,
this can be applied tooooooo
Bad vibes

(from *EXTRAVAGANZA DELUXE!*)

Blackout

There's a lack of light
in the sky tonight
What a pretty sight
Blackout

Candlesticks were lit
Couples made a kid
Thank the power grid
Blackout

Things like this
don't happen 'round here very often
Just goes to show you how repetitive
repetitive
repetitive
repetitive
repetitive
repetitive
repetitive
our life is

There's a lack of light
in the sky tonight
What a pretty sight
Blackout

(from *Game Show Teeth*)

Blues In My Beer

Blues in my beer, red's in my eye
Dark in my thoughts, darken the sky
Blues in my beer

When we tied the knot,
not a minute could go on without her
It's been a very long alcoholic journey I've been on

We thought our marriage was stashed away
under the piles of powder and dust
But as I reflect and look down at myself,
I can now see what uncovered us

And now that my ship's come in,
I can't stop thinking about her

Blues in my beer, red's in my eye
Cash in my thoughts, embark on this life

(from *pOp cOrn*)

Boan-Ga-Loar

Boan-ga-loar
Boan-ga-loar
Wee-no-see-shee-eet-no-moar

Wair-shee-hyde
Wair-shee-hyde
Shee-no-hyde-shee-tearn-tue-syde

No-wan-fude
Shee-bee-sik
Oan-lee-hed-bee-thing-dat-thik

Boan-ga-loar
Boan-ga-loar
Whye-doo-yoo-no-eet-no-moar?

Boan-ga-loar
Boan-ga-loar
Yes-tue-day-shee-moan-no-moar

(from *pOp cOrn*)

Brother Nature

Brother nature's playing a game for the ages
He's shuffling the pages of history
Brother nature's playing a game for the ages
He's hustling contagious in mystery

Branches of the trees are veins
that flow with water from another time
Rivers are resilient
Clouds are proud
Grass is gregarious
Nature's jigsaw puzzle
patchwork fields the heavens' checkerboard in mime
Wind is the invisible game piece
Humans are notorious for cheating

Birds will swirl and swerve
mixed in a cocktail of the fog and moon and stars
Hills and valleys just a carpet
to cover past mistakes in strategy
Unassuming animals
are wise to all the secrets of the sun
Stormy skies bluff above
Natural catastrophes up the ante

Brother nature's playing a game for the ages
He's shuffling the pages of history
Brother nature's playing a game for the ages
He's rustling outrageous in mystery

(from *FRED*)

Can't Spend a Cent

When it's gotten to the point
where you can't spend a cent,
and you think about the pennies
and the nickels that you lent
to a bum or a chum or a well-to-do gent
Keep your head up
Don't get fed up

So the jangle of your pocket
is down to just a clink?
There are many people like you
who would simply start to think
of a myriad of methods to acquire food and drink
But of course you'll
be resourceful

If fancy food's your fancy, well you just give it up
That sterling silver knife and fork is now a small tin cup
Yes begging can be chancy, but never become timid
A song and dance on knees and hands
and all the sky's the limit!

Give every species on the Earth
some fit and ample funding
and humankind would snatch it all,
and think that it was cunning
The truth is that no dog or cat
or bird or fish would want it,
while people try to keep all that they can,
and even flaunt it

(unrecorded)

Car Rap

Car
fuel injection
jerk choke
clutch choke choke jerk choke choke jerk
clutch exhaust stall flat

Speed honk honk honk cruise crawl park
inspection   -   -   -   antenna
pump inflate pump pump inflate
pump inflate pump pump
Blowout blowout
pump inflate pump pump die

Jumpstart battery
shock charge hesitate . . . inspect gauge BEEP BEEP
shock charge inspect gauge BEEP BEEP BEEP BEEP
Starter motor cruise control

(from *pOp cOrn*)

Chants of Rain

Buckets, buckets
Cats and dogs
Wet the meadows into bogs
Rain enough to float some logs
Buckets, buckets
Cats and dogs

Buckets, buckets
Cats and dogs
Soak the lilies for the frogs
Make a mud bath for the hogs
Buckets, buckets
Cats and dogs

(from *EXTRAVAGANZA DELUXE!*)

Clickin' and Surfin'

I'm clickin' and surfin', I'm circlin' the earth and
I used to be human, now I'm a mouse
I'm watchin' my modem slowly downloadin',
thinking that one day I may leave the house
I'm thinking that some day I may leave the house

I'm reading through emails, weeding through females
looking for someone who speaks the same font
This digital flirting is so disconcerting
An analog girlfriend is all that I want
An analog girlfriend is all that I want

So tcpipppisdnter.com
http:/ backlash ad nauseam

I'm sittin' and frettin' but still internettin'
as java and jpegs jump from the screen
As dollars are debting, my appetite's whetting
The fee for such access ain't all that's obscene
If only they had this when I was thirteen!

I'm clickin' and surfin'

(from *The Importance of Sauce*)

Color Feel

Green gets me green with envy
Blue makes me blue
Red and I'm more than ready to be like you
Yellow and all my fellow senses warm up
Aquamarine is sunscreen to make them stop

See the best I get is a color feel
and colors feel alright
Yeah the best I get is a color feel
and colors feel out of sight!

Now I know that the world is not so
black and white for real
'Cause the colors
Oh the colors
Yeah the colors,
How good they feel, oh . . .

Pink if a tulip and a tool looked the same?
Orange you glad an orange looks like its name?
Brown and I'm bround to groan and feel like dirt
Purple's purplexing and makes me want to blurt

If the best you get is a color feel
Well colors feel alright
Yeah the best I get is a color feel
and colors feel out of sight!

Color Feel Color Feel Color Feel Color

(from *Purple Burt*)

Comfort Zone

I'm standing alone in this comfort zone,
behind the boundary
The only decree in this comfort zone
is to live consistently
I say what I want in this comfort zone
with no one judging me
No worry, no stress as I sit at home
sipping some herbal tea

Ideas come up
Words come out,
fitting into expectations
Safety first will make it last
This could be my ruination

It's time to break out of this comfort zone
and push myself to the edge
I'm nervous about everything unknown
I bet is over that ledge
Working outside of this comfort zone
is difficult I'm sure
It might be exciting to be shown
parts of me not seen before

Alerts go out
Alarms go off
Lights go on along the fences
I climb up
I jump down,
and sprint to grab hold of my senses

Where's the challenge in nonchalance?
Where's the fun in fussiness?
There's just famine in the familiar
There's no party in being particular
It's way too convenient to stay oh-so lenient on myself

Finally gone from that comfort zone,
there's danger in every move
Exhilaration I've never known,
and so much room to improve
Success might be less than in comfort zones
but confidence is much more
I used to be scared to ever roam,
now I can't wait to explore

(from *SING SING*)

Contagious

We are contagious
to what the latest rage is
Contagious
for nits of all ages

Is it a sickness?
Or just a thickness?
We've got to lick this
free will killer

Contagious
gets on all the pages
Contagious
Let's lock 'em up in cages

Why do we latch on
to the latest fashion?
This disease will catch on
in the right atmosphere, but

You're probably immune
if you didn't swoon
for hula hoops and pet rocks
Leisure suits and wood clogs

We are contagious
in different stages
With an infection
of predilection for trash

It's not bacteria
so just be leery of
little urges for
spending splurges

Start with a quarantine
on Florentine art snobs,

foreign teen heartthrobs
and home shopping mart slobs

It hits you if it fits you
The fever grows because it knows who to pursue
Let's give it the old one-two punch
No more "Let's do lunch"

If you're contagious
try to save your wages
and be the first one on your block
to last

(from *HENWAY - Big Hair*)

Crack The Case

Opportunity knocks on my door
after twenty years on the local force
I will show what my badge is for
Here's my chance to even the score
No more duty at a desk
I will rise above the rest
'Cause this time, yeah this time
I will crack the case
alone
I will crack the case

Promotion's a notion
that is foremost in my mind
when I solve this crime

These criminals are no match for me
Thinking fast will be the key
The FBI's a bureaucracy
I'll handle this personally
No more paperwork at night
Decoration's in my sight
Because this time, yeah this time
I will crack the case
alone
I will crack the case

Emotion's a potion
I am feeling energized
Lead me to the prize

Because this time, yeah this time
I will crack the case
alone
I will crack the case

(from *Game Show Teeth*)

Dear So & So

You like to go on an ego excursion
First class diversion, no fare for me
Turbulence does help to pilot your brain plane
to see the brain pain fuming from me

Concede conceit, admit defeat
You wrote the note to Dear So & So
Dear So & So and so on
Concede conceit, admit defeat
You wrote the note to Dear So & So

You mustn't think
"I'll let him know, he'll let me go.
The letter goes out tonight."
But you smudge your ink and continue to think
"He's way below me."
I'm on the brink so don't try to phone me, phoney

We might just go on but you need coersion
from me, urgently, so you'll care for me

Concede conceit, admit defeat
You wrote the note to Dear So & So

And so on and so on, we might just go on
but you need coersion, first class

(from *pOp cOrn*)

Dinner For None

"Welcome. Tonight's dinner consists of
chocolate-covered spinach and licorice pizza
hors d'oeuvres, gingerly dipped in breadcrumbs,
Tabasco sauce and vanilla ice cream, sandwiched
between warm lettuce leaves dripping with chicken fat
and served on Oreos for an appetizer.

For the main course - Congealed meatloaf and prune
soup paste, lopped over a raw bacon slab stuffed with
bubble gum and whipped cream, then gently deep-fried
in year-old oil with sand.

Served with side orders of - Cold dry spaghetti mousse
floating in cream cheese and orange juice,
and a small dish of steamed Saltines.

For dessert, a choice of the following - Scrambled eggs
with shells in banana Jello, or raw clam meringue pie.
Chiclets and candy corn frozen in beer,
a fresh cannoli filled with plaque,
or a refreshing glass of chilled urine."

(from *EXTRAVAGANZA DELUXE!* and *The Importance of Sauce*)

Do The Milkshake

Do the milkshake
Yes it do
Feel the ground quake? It's me, Moo-Moo!

Why stand alone in a field
chewing on a mouthful of grass,
when I could spring around like a ping pong ball
and afterwards fill up a glass?

I do the milkshake
It's not a dance
You simply can't fake ants in your pants

People have a beef with me
because I'm fat and make lots of noise
But my udders would make butter if I just did the twist
which is not a drink for most girls and boys

I do the milkshake
Don't ask for skim
It's not what I make - Do I look slim?

Dairy, dairy, quite ordinary
How does your party go?
Well with Moo-Moo bouncing over the moon,
my shake will taste out of this world,
and happiness lasts all afternoon

Do the milkshake
Yes it does
Oh how my feet ache
Well that's because . . .

I'm a bouncing cow!

(from *Purple Burt*)

Do-Re-Mimi

There you are, you look so pretty
Here I am, oh why can't we be
side by side with every new day?
When you're near the world is okay

I'll be yours until the end of
time because we are so in love
Though the news is sad you're bringing
nothing will keep me from singing

Do-Re-Mimi, I love you
sing so sweetly
and have a beauty few
have ever seen, even in dreams
Do-Re-Mimi

They say that out of sight is out of mind
Call me crazy but the more I think of you I'm fine

(Purple Burt, I love you)

Far away but right here with me
In my brain your face I can see
Even now as time is ticking,
you're the girl that I am picking

Do-Re-Mimi, I love you
and me we
are one made up of two-
gether, forever
Do-Re-Mimi

Do-Re-Mimi
Fe-li-city

(from *Purple Burt*)

Don't Get The Gods Mad

Your superiors
have one up on you
All that fear of yours
powers what they do
in your behalf

Beings in the clouds,
give one more chance to me
Someday you'll be proud
of my piety
I swear, this time

Don't get the gods mad . . .

Just ask the masters
what they do for their pleasure
Some of those bastards dole out doom
in their leisure time

I want food and love,
that's why this baby cries
Mom and dad above me,
I'm the apple in your eyes
but kids grow rotten

Could you tell the boss
I won't be coming in?
I need the day off
after last night's drinking binge
He won't miss me

Don't get the gods mad . . .

Once upon a time all mortal men lived as equals
It is a crime some lesser guy wrote the sequel book

Mr. Movie Star,
may I take your photograph?
Suppose we expose
your whole darker half
with my camera?

It is judgment day
for our special family
Do just what I say
and live for eternity
You must trust me

Don't get the gods mad . . .

(from *The Importance of Sauce*)

Don't Hold a Grudge

When we talk you're much too picky
which makes the situation sticky
which gets me stuck in all those tricky
games you say I play with you

All those notions in your noggin
keep on, keep on, keep on boggin'
down my chances of uncloggin'
both the lobes you listen through

Don't hold a grudge
Don't hold a grudge
Don't hold a grudge
All it is is mental sludge

When we talk you're much too picky
which makes the situation sticky
which gets me stuck in all those tricky
games you say I play with you

All those notions in your noggin
keep on, keep on, keep on cloggin'
those emotions which are boggin'
down my words like Super Glue

Don't hold a grudge
Don't hold a grudge
Don't hold a grudge
All it is is mental sludge

I can't regret what i haven't said
I can't regret what i haven't said
I can't regret what i haven't said
yet

Don't hold a grudge
Don't hold a grudge

Don't hold a grudge
You've got to learn to budge

I forgive and I forget
but I am easily reminded
you've reasoned that I've treasoned
which ain't pleasin' either of us

(from *pOp cOrn*)

Everything Makes Me Cry

Men should be tough like Paul Bunyon
These days my life's a big sliced onion

It's good to well up with emotion
Get a load of my facial ocean

I try to be a sensitive guy
but these days everything makes me cry

Wonder if there's something scientific
about my tear ducts being so prolific?

I'm always on the verge of bawling
Bing Bong, it's Mitchie Faye Baker calling

I try to be a sensitive guy
but these days everything makes me cry

Sniffles end up as a slobber
Smiley me is close to sobber

It's not just depressed, sometimes it's ecstatic
This soggy salty mess is almost automatic

I try to be a sensitive guy
but these days everything makes me cry

(unrecorded)

Fairy Tale

Once upon a time in a land far away,
there lived a couple who was happy and gay
The couple knew they were taking a chance
"What will they think? We both wear the pants."

Very nearby lived a grouchy, rich man
who got all his money from leasing his land
"How dare that couple be happy that way!
Besides the rent, how shall they pay?"

Each day he watched them through the trees
"They have a filthy mind disease!"
The man soon vowed to set them straight
or free their minds, at any rate

"The sooner the better," the man proclaimed
"Your kind of animal must be tamed."

The couple moved to somewhere else
The man had ruined their mental health

The moral to this story is:
The object of life is to be able to live

(from *EXTRAVAGANZA DELUXE!*)

Flavor Day

There's a day that's almost here,
it's oh so near that I can taste it
Grab yourself some sweet and sour,
in one hour celebrate it
No need to anticipate a reason to salivate
Oh so many treats a'plenty piled on your plate

Flavor day
Flavor day is here!

Flavor day comes only once a year
Everyone stick out your tongue and cheer!
(Yay!)

How about a mustard-covered,
salty, spicy ice cream sundae?
It may taste ridiculous
but why not try on such a fun day?
Everything is yummy now
but your mouth's too full to "Wow!"
Swallow soon and make more room
for scrumptious fun chow

Flavor day
Flavor day is here!

Flavor day comes only once a year
Everyone stick out your tongue and cheer!
(Yay!)

(from *Purple Burt*)

From Soup To Nuts

The irony is that we started out
as nothing more than some pond scum
Now we're erect and derelict,
that simple slime seems much more handsome
We're a detestable festival
celebrating brainlessness
Way back when, we had no brains
to get us into such a mess

We've gone from soup to nuts
From goop to putz
Blame it on mutation
From molecules to shallow fools
Darwin's getting impatient

When once a word sprung from our lips
it changed the course of evolution
Today those lips go unsung
unless they're plumped like a seat cushion
Childbirth was risky business,
dangerous for mom and baby
Now an infant smokes three packs
Aborting adults needs a maybe

We've gone from soup to nuts
From goop to mutts
Blame it on mutation
From proteinase to a disgrace
Darwin's getting impatient

Primordial to mortifying
Chemical to comical
Single cell to simpleminded
How did we grow from amino acids
to mean old asses?

We've gone from soup to nuts
From goop to butts
Blame it on mutation
From dinosaur to wino whore
Darwin's getting impatient

You'd never know to get to now
it has taken beyond eons
From afar on some dark star,
we're flashing neon as mere peons

(from *SING SING*)

Gibberish

Baby buckets
Pink wall sockets
Bathtubs filled with smelly jelly

Grass stains
Gas pains
A striped shirt with no holes

Whadya' say?
Come again?
Not for puppies only

How about a see-thru flag?
A bag lady in her bag

Doctor, lawyer, garbage man
Dollar bills in a can

Soup's up
Temp's down
The prison wants a birthday clown

Gibberish gibberish
Words from where there are no fish
Golly gee, ain't she a dish?
Huh?

(unrecorded)

Halfway to Heaven

There's no need for religion if you've got but a smidgen
of belief in where you're going once you're bones
So don't call your creator, he'll just say "See you later"
and leave you with a thunderous dial tone

Ever since the Big Bang, a spirit called the yin-yang
has blurred the line between what's bad and good
Abnormal didn't fit so they labeled me a schizo
I'd love to kill them but I'm not in the mood

I'm only halfway to heaven
Like bread that's unleavened
I need much more than time to help me rise
So while I say hello to hell and wish the devil well,
please save me a seat up in the sky

It's cloudy where I'm goin'
and down here we're all glowin'
I hope my tan is showin' on the day that I arrive

Part of me's an angel, the rest of me's derangelled
This was tabulated when I died
If only I'd been nicer instead of trying to ice her
my wingtips wouldn't be here getting fried

Before I climb this ladder, I better clear my bladder
'cause it's a mighty distance to ascend
It won't be such a long wait if no one's guarding the gate,
assuming I can get the bars to bend

I'm only halfway to heaven
Like bread that's unleavened
I need much more than time to help me rise
So while I say hello to hell and wish the devil well,
please save me a seat up in the sky

(from *FRED*)

Hazy Recollection

Who knew what and when did they know it?

How can you expect me to recall
who I screwed over twenty years ago?
It was only yesterday I screwed some more
and even they I don't know

It seems I've got an image problem
but my rep will see it through
I've got no time for such nonsense,
that's what she's paid to do

In my hazy recollection I've done nothing wrong
One day this crazy press obsession
is bound to move along

When you're as important as this guy,
you might feel some empathy
The public's like bugs 'round a pig sty,
and FYI, that pig's not me

It is open to interpretation
what is legal involving me
That is a determination
often made once we agree on your fee

I've been to rehab five times over
That's commitment to be clean
Common people eat this stuff up
from what I can glean

In my hazy recollection I've done nothing wrong
Each day this lazy guilt connection
helps me to grow strong
It's me against the throng

(from *SING SING*)

Hope-Rope It!

Wanna fly like a bird?
Hope-Rope it!
Wanna spell every word?
Hope-Rope it!
Be a Hollywood star?
Hope-Rope it!
Play a monkey guitar?
Hope-Rope it!

If there's anything that you want to be
Want to know, have, do, or would love to see
Then grab these handles and jump with glee
'cause it might happen instantly
if you Hope-Rope it!

Announcer: The Hope-Rope by Magiko!
(Sneakers sold separately)

(from *Purple Burt*)

I Hate Love

Take a look at her
I feel very weak
Beauty does that stuff
when you try to speak
I'm in love with her
Simple as can be
She's in love with him
Where does that leave me?

You broke my heart
I am in pain
Next time I might get
to ask your name
All my life I've looked
for the perfect mate
I can't be a real good catch
when I'm using sour bait

I hate love when I'm not in it
I hate love when I am
I hate love
What a scam

Men and women are
meant for one another
To have, to hold,
to hurt, to deceive,
just like father did to mother
Why do we look
for the real thing,
when we all know deep, deep down
it's just a worthless brass ring?

I hate love when I'm not in it
I hate love when I am
I hate love
What a scam

You always want what you don't have
and now you've got it,
get rid of it
The more time that you search for love,
the harder it is to keep every bit of it

I hate love

Sex is not love
Fun is not love
A kiss is not love
A hug is not love
A laugh is not love
A cry is not love
Money's not love
Time is not love

Love is love is love is love

I hate love

(rough demo)

I Have Never Lied

I have never lied to anyone,
that kind of thing is done by liars
I have never lied to anyone,
that was my brother who yelled "Fire!"

Everything I've ever said is true
Especially all the things I said to you
If I ever lied to anyone
I would know because I'm honest

I have never cried to anyone,
that kind of thing is done by babies
I have never cried to anyone,
no matter how absorbent they be

Every tear I'll ever shed, I'd hide
This is really easy when you stay inside
If I ever cried to anyone
I would laugh because I'm lying

I swear to tell the whole truth
and nothing but the truth, so help me God,
but I'm left-handed

I will never side with anyone,
that kind of thing is done by losers
I will never side with anyone,
who said that beggars can't be choosers?

All opinions people have are wrong,
except, of course, the ones that you hear in this song
If I ever side with anyone
it's because I cleaned my mirror

I will never die for anyone,
that kind of thing is done by people

I will never die for anyone,
just to eat dirt beneath a steeple

Every minute I'm alive will be
a new chance to hear my name read on TV
If I ever die for anyone
they had better take full credit

(from *Game Show Teeth*)

I Hope

Rope goes round and round
It hits the ground and makes a clicking sound
As feet go up and down
and down and up and down and up and down

I hope I see my Do-Re-Mimi soon again,
so she can sing me a pretty tune again
I hope my daddy will come back to me again,
so we can throw a ball and crawl near sea again

I hope . . .

Jumping rope is not just excellent exercise
If you hope, great things may appear before your eyes

I hope I become visible to everyone,
and finally experience most every fun
I hope I'll see some colors one day very soon
so I can enjoy all that blooms in early June

I hope . . .

(from *Purple Burt*)

I Miss My Daddy

I miss my daddy so very badly
Now that he's gone away
he'll always stay in my memory

We had such fun once
Father and son months
when we would throw a ball
or crawl across the beach on our knees

He could be funny, smart or mean
He could wear fancy suits or jeans
He could cook eggs or eat sardines
Like you or me he was just a human being

So tell your daddy you love him and see
how much he loves you back
You'll never lack the thing you need most

You should be glad he is your own daddy
'cause if he leaves like mine
you'll find how much it meant to be close

I miss him

(from *Purple Burt*)

I Need a Hug

I need a hug
I need to snuggle-up
To feel the warmth that will bubble up
when people double up
I need a hug

I'm not speaking of sex
and I'm not talking 'bout kissing
The squeeze and the relax
is what I have been missing

I need a hug
I need to cuddle-up
into a two person huddle-up
to make all my trouble stop
I need a hug

'Cause no amount of beer to chug
nor snappy, happy, crappy drug
could send my emotions to the ceiling
like the up-uplifting feeling
of a hug

To feel as snug as a bug in a rug
would really tug my heart strings
But just some old fuddy-duddy won't do
It must be some buddy's body, like you

I need a hug

(from *EXTRAVAGANZA DELUXE!*)

I See You

I see you seeing me
I see me seeing thee

I'm a 20/20 something guy
with a whole lotta lovely in my eyes
closed wishing that we were kissing
They open and we are

I see you seeing me
I see us saying we

All kidding aside, here's looking at you
Clearly I'm hoping you share my view
through glasses half full and tinted
with shades and hues of blush

Focus on the future if you can
Make your past a blur
Hocus pocus sleight of hand in hand
A him to her

(from *The Importance of Sauce*)

I Wish I Was a Kid Again

I wish I could begin again
Let information in again
To be naturally thin again
And feel real close to kin again
To dread the medicine again
And make a healthy din again
I wish, I wish, I wish, I wish, I wish
I wish I was a kid again

I'd like to start brand new again
Before I ever grew again
To gurgle, spit and coo again
And sing "The Cow Goes Moo" again
The first time to the zoo again
Read *Horton Hears a Who!* again
I wish, I wish, I wish, I wish, I wish
I wish I was brand new again

If I knew now what I didn't know then
I wouldn't be right where I am
I wish, I wish, I wish, I wish I was a kid again

I wish I was a lad again
Spend more time with my dad again
To not know good from bad again
A nursery school grad again
Just crayons and a pad again
Wear pants and shirt both plaid again
I wish, I wish, I wish, I wish, I wish
I wish I was a lad again

I want to be a boy again
To not have to act coy again
To wear clothes by Rob Roy again
And hear grandma say "Oy!" again
To play with my new toy again
And hear the song "Convoy" again

I wish, I wish, I wish, I wish, I wish
I wish I was a boy again

You can't redo your childhood
but sometimes dreaming's twice as good
I wish, I wish, I wish, I wish I was a kid again

I wish I was a tyke again
Boys and girls look alike again
My first "condenser mic" again
Go on a Cub Scout hike again
To ride my little bike again
Get scared and yell out "Yikes!" again
I wish, I wish, I wish, I wish, I wish
I wish I was a tyke again

I wish I was a child again
The height of juveniled again
Not care how hair is styled again
And watch the *Kingdom Wild* again
To march in single file again
And be newly beguiled again
I wish, I wish, I wish, I wish, I wish
I wish I was a child again

Some people never, ever grow up,
but who doesn't love a pup?
I wish, I wish, I wish, I wish I was a kid again

I wish my slate was clean again
Much younger than preteen again
When nude was not obscene again
And eat a new Peek Frean again
Read *Highlights* magazine again
When all was peachy keen again
I wish, I wish, I wish, I wish, I wish
I wish my slate was clean again

I wish I could begin again
To knock down just one pin again
To watch the Mets' big win again
And swim with fears of fin again
To laugh at Gilligan again
And see my first Chaplin again
I wish, I wish, I wish, I wish, I wish I was a kid again
I wish, I wish, I wish, I wish, I wish I was a kid

(from *FRED*)

I'm Gonna Rock My Baby Tonight

I'm gonna rock, rock, rock my baby tonight
I'm gonna treat my, treat my, baby right

I'm gonna crank her tunes and make like a clown
Then I'll cradle her when the sun goes down

They say her talk is mostly dribble
but she's alright when she starts to scribble

I'm gonna rock, rock, rock my baby tonight
I'm gonna rock her till she's pink and blue
I'm gonna treat my, treat my baby right
If you rock hard you could have one too

She turns me on with her high-pitched shrills
When she warms my heart she give me chills

My baby wouldn't be a crier
if I couldn't pacify her

I'm gonna rock, rock, rock my baby tonight
I'm gonna rock her in the morning light
I know my baby'll be alright
as long as she's in my sight
tonight

(from *EXTRAVAGANZA DELUXE!*)

Ice Me Nice

Before the big melt,
I'm gonna find my favorite pelt
and shuffle up this climate change deck we've been dealt
A future of sweat is something I would soon regret
To try a cryogenic nap seems my best bet
Comfort comes at a pretty price,
so flick the switch
and ice me nice

The waters may rise,
tornadoes might spin from the skies
Not me, I won't be party to such a surprise
You think that I'm bent for laying out decades of rent
If those rays are just a phase it will be money well spent
Set my alarm for paradise,
then flick the switch
and ice me nice

I dig the change of seasons as much as the other guy
but I'm swapping old for cold
so wake me up after the fry

Don't jot my obit,
to do this you gotta have grit
I'm claustrophobic and you won't see me throw a fit
Just keep me separate from the mice,
then flick the switch and ice me nice
Yeah, flick the switch and ice me nice

(from *SING SING*)

If Every Day Was Christmas

If every day was Christmas
there would be no more crime
An automatic, everlasting peace in our time

If every day was Christmas
there would be no more hate,
and the world would be just great!

If every day
If every day
If every day
was Christmas

Christmas, Christmas
stay a little while
Christmas, Christmas
put a great big smile
on the face
of the human race,
for the rest of the year

Could every day be Christmas?
In your dreams my dear
For Christmas is a time of cheer
just one day a year

Should every day be Christmas
just think of all the fun
Pum puh pum pum pum pum pun!

(from *FRED*)

In The Know

Ever since the days of primary school,
been jealous of the ways
of the smart and the cool
Casually first, always with the last word
I wish I had a ticket to hear what they heard

Now I have a job and I'm needing a raise
A couple of my cronies receive all the praise
They're fast with facts and figures,
I'm beat to the punch
It's slightly more than insight
or heavenly hunch

You're heading in the right direction
Turn left at the intersection
of Social Circle and Easy Way
Spy the light bulb and entree'

In the know
A secret spot for those who run the show
In the know
Where fortunes and reputations grow
Oh my son you've been blessed
with info you could never guess

Promising stocks, shipments at docks
Winning horses, cheap divorces, easy bosses
Passwords and codes, discounted clothes
Special tables, lower taxes,
Free cable, backstage access

Power is a privilege some would abuse
Taking full advantage as a Who's Who
Being an insider is all that I need
A life of peace and pleasure
would be guaranteed

Good evening sir, may I remind you
that your ID is your IQ?
Our main course is microfiche
but first won't you enjoy some quiche?

In the know
Where the fancy and the future famous go
In the know
The most important word you'll hear's "Hello"
Throw your past life away
From now on you'll need to stay
in the know

(from *Game Show Teeth*)

Indian Giver

She was his young squaw and he was her scout
They consummating
They consummating
He ask to marry and she be so proud
No hesitating
No hesitating

Smoke signals billow above their bedroom
Near tribes receive it
Near tribes receive it
Has not been such howling in many a moon
Foxes come heed it
Foxes come heed it

She paint her face up while his skin get red
She add a war stripe
She add a war stripe
She catch him wearing a dress on his head
She smash the peace pipe
She smash the peace pipe

The creep, he built a teepee for his sweet pea, now she weepie

Oh oh oh
Indian giver
No no
Indian giver
Oh oh
Indian giver

He gave her his heart then he take it away
Now she do rain dance
Now she do rain dance
He think that life is a dear hunting game
Now she do war chants
Now she do war chants

The creep, he built a teepee for his sweet pea,
now she weepie

Oh oh oh
Indian giver
No no
Indian giver
Oh oh
Indian giver

Giving gift, a sacred act
Making rift when take it back
If you miffed then fist do pack
Spirit lift if face you smack

He promise warmth but he only do pelt her
Now she crying a river
Now she crying a river
One man for two women is too fertile delta
She need your skin back so she no more shiver

The creep, he built a teepee for his sweet pea,
now she weepie

Oh oh oh
Indian giver

He gave her his heart then he take it away

(from *The Importance of Sauce*)

Indoor Wildlife

Saw a mouse in my apartment last night
Asked him "Where you goin' partner?"
He said "Home, home under the range
My campfire is your pilot light
Crumbs and drips the only fodder
so please choose cheese for a change"
Hey, suddenly I'm Gulliver on my own grange

Indoor wildlife
Not your ideal tableaux
Rather be a hobo
then sit and squirm in urban vermin

Rats and roaches grazing on some garbage
as fluffy dust balls roll by
Spiders hanging out in homemade hammocks
in a corner of the sky
A hundred-watt sun beats down on the hardwood floor
A caravan of ants surround a sandwich
like they're above the law

Set some traps in my apartment today
Start of critter lynching season
Black flag flying with pride
Revolting in this home of the brave
is the vilest kind of treason
so die by insecticide
Hey, putting my foot down has got me gratified

Indoor wildlife
Not your ideal tableaux
Rather be a hobo
then sit and squirm in urban vermin

(from *The Importance of Sauce*)

Invisibility

Close your eyes and look at me
That's invisibility
Open them and look around
I am nowhere to be found
So you wanna shake my hand?
First you must know where I am
Step right up, turn on the light
I'm completely out of sight

Where did he go? Where did he go?
Where did he go? Where'd he go?

I may be big, I may be small
I may not be here at all
I sneak in to things for free
Thank invisibility
Peek a boo, I see you
Too bad you can't see me too
Play hide and seek? You wouldn't dare
I'm not here, there, anywhere

Where did he go? Where did he go?
Where did he go? Where'd he go?

Life is often fantastic
when you are a magic trick
Mirror, mirror on the wall,
who's the clearest of them all?

Invisibil . . . . ity!
Invisibil . . . . ity!
Invisibil . . . . ity!
Invisible . . . . That's me!

(from *Purple Burt*)

Is Love There?

I went to San Francisco in the summertime
and all I found was chilly fog and lonely hearts
If all you need is in the air like oxygen
then what's this crazy little thing
called that stinks?

So is love there?
Where is love, where?

You'll find some in that actress Hewitt's middle name
Connect with it on Chuck Woolery's TV game
Add a 'g' and enter baseball's Hall of Fame
This silly song is getting lame

I took a radar roller coaster to a jungle shack
The only thing for keeping was a boat for sale

So is love there? (It was but it's not)
Where is love, where? (It's not where it was)

They say the look of it is in your eyes (two times)
But you're just drunk on potion #9 (on the rocks)

(from *FRED*)

It Won't Be Long Now

I was born with primo genes
which make my bottom and top clean
What goes up must come down
but only one end wears a frown

Hair today and gone tomorrow
I'll keep giving you some skin
Heading for happiness, not sorrow
Bald is how we all begin
So shield your eyes while I take a bow
It won't be long now

Telly, Mr. Clean and Yul
used their shiny, skin smooth tool
to coax the women through their doors
for hot romance and cleaner floors

The gentle egg sits there in the shade
It had no trouble getting laid
Look at Gandhi and Sinead
The masses say they got it made
and neither of them had a cow
It won't be long now

Minoxodil is nearly nil
Rugs and weaves are worser still
Transplants you can just forget,
my skull is not some Chia Pet

No need to spray, cut, style or primp
No colorings or permanents
Throw brushes, combs, and driers out
A lesser man would sit and pout
We'd all be better off this way
All people white, black, yellow or gray
would be more similar today
So shave it off now, don't delay!

Barbers are barbarians,
cutting off what's right for them
Some surgery they used to do
so count your ears,
there should be two

There's plenty more in other places
Some is pubic, some is public
The stuff that grows out of my face is
such a nag, I keep it stubbly

Just comb it back from your brow
It won't be long now
Even Buddha got you ta' bow and cow-tow
It won't be long now

(unrecorded)

Keep It a Secret

From your bowl of Oatie-O's
Benny Banana whispered a warning
You leaned in and listening,
filled up your mouth and mind through the morning
If all that he told you is all that you told me,
my advice to you would be to

Keep it a secret
Someone might kill you for that
Keep it a secret

What if it got out?
What if it ran?
Just stick your tongue out
and trip it up while you can

History spins like a dish
atop a pole on the Sullivan show
If infamy is not your wish,
give it a nudge while it's teetering slowly
The future of mankind and possibly more
all depends on if you choose to

Keep it a secret
Someone might love you for that
Keep it a secret

Is it a rumor?
Is it a plan?
Would food use humor
to stick it to the man?

From your bowl of Oatie-O's
Barry Blueberry mumbled good morning . . .

(from *Game Show Teeth*)

Kloreen

Kloreen,
with eyes of pools of blue
Your sheen,
a gentle lilting hue

Let me dive into your sea of blond
hair-like, snare-like gentle frond,
to beat a backstroke on beyond
the sun soaked horizon,
with your eyes on me

Kloreen,
with eyes of pools of blue
Young queen,
a purpose to pursue

Let me float my little body boat
by your purring, furry throat
A girlish whirlpool where I tote
my tension revolving,
dissolving from a scree

Eighty bathing beauties from the movies
could not match your aqua-spectacular

Raindrops rebound in triplicate
Teardrops trickling are tickling it
Sunspots grapple to evaporate
Paramecium populate
No activity of this nature
throws pacifity from your stature

Kloreen,
I'm keen on you

(from *HENWAY - Big Hair* and *FRED*)

La Bomba

No, no, no droppa la bomba
You will kill all of de mamas if you do dis thing
And all de people be somba
since one will not be de numba where de freedom ring
So children sing
this plea we bring

Cop la bomba
Flop la bomba
Stop la bomba
Calm la bomb

No try to toppa la bomba
Save all of de mula and shoppa for fellow man
Buy food and fuel to be proppa
We can be a coopa-rating land
So all join hands
So all join hands and

Cop la bomba
Flop la bomba
Stop la bomba
Calm la bomb

No, no, no droppa la bomba

(from *EXTRAVAGANZA DELUXE!*)

Laura

We met a day before the war
Not a shot had fired
We met two weeks after my personal ad expired
You thought I'd just check you out
instead of going to meet ya'
But I was eying cream cheese
and not a piece of pizza

Laura, Laura
You mean so much more to me
than some Israeli Torah
Laura, Laura
In thirty years I'll take you hand
for in richer or in poorer
Laura, Laura
I'll be with you forever, one day

In six months we have grown together
Talking gave way to kissing
Our passions heated like the weather
Shivering became shvitzing
The future soon will be the past
The hourglass sands are sliding
Don't worry darling, I'll be with you
sure as Henry will be biting

Hair up, hair down,
hair up, hair down

Laura, you're a
beautiful girl from the outside
right down to your core-a
Laura, Laura
Half a year, but the time of my life

Foodie Feedie becomes Chucky
Eat tahini, muffins shmuckie

Piece of squid is very yucky
Jogging past "Beware of Duckies"

Henry, Bingo, La and Cody
Ferry, paddle and rowboatie
Amber waves and Answer Me
Monster faces, A&E

Miniature golf, the St. Rita
Food's not that good, eat a pita
I'm sorry, are you sure?
Pointing funny, driving poor

After *Alice* walking home
Silly voices, I hate foam
Take the train to Allenhurst
Laughing loud then lips are pursed

New York Press, t-shirt dress
Baseball cap, cactus sap
Pacific northwest, turkey breast
Fresh espresso, too much pesto

Rita, Betty, Carl and Doris
Cherry tomatoes from Morris
Poop deck door, lunge for sauce
Friday chores, weekday course

Bathtub meal, babaganouchie,
Son of the lake catching sushi
AV directors, *I Love Lucy*
I just blacked out, ass is squooshie

A back scratchy, fall asleepie,
Goofy Q-tips, lots of pee pee
Etc., etc., etc.

They say that good things come
to those who wait

The best thing ever was our first date
Pasta blah blah, Cafe' Sha Sha

Laura, Laura
You're everything I ever dreamed of
and a whole lot more-a
Laura, Laura
What a girl, what a girlfriend you are

Tickling, grunting,
kneading, dunking

Laura, Laura
I love you

(from *FRED*)

Let Me Be Your Pet

Let me be your pet
Think of all the love you'd get
Even after learning tricks
like doing flips and fetching sticks
I promise to be loyal, assuming royal treatment

Let me be your pet
I think of all the food I'd get
Even if I'm unable
to put my paws on the table
I know that I'll get your attention as a family extension

Let me be your pet
Put me on videocassette
with all of your relations
and family vacations,
for everyone to treasure all that gives you pleasure

Like a dog with a smile or a cat in basket,
I'll belong to you even while in the casket

Let me be your pet
to use me when you get upset,
and holler out my dumb nickname
because you are the one to blame
Forgetting to let me out and finding my mess all about

Get another pet
This relationship's all wet
I don't need my instincts
to sniff out what stinks
I hope it won't unnerve you to know I observe you

Let me be your pet

(from *HENWAY - Big Hair*)

Little Masterpiece

The painter places her final stroke
then slowly steps back so to soak in
every inch of her work of art,
full of all of her soul and heart

That's my little masterpiece
A brand new creative release
From me to you
From me to you
Yeah, me to you

The new momma nurses her baby boy
You know he's her perfect pride and joy
As she suckles her first son
she thinks "He's the best thing I've ever done"

He's my little masterpiece
A brand new creative release
From me to you
From me to you
Yeah, me to you

A new planet now complete
so God kicks up his tired feet
There's resources and room to roam,
so all you dwellers, welcome home!

Use my little masterpiece
A brand new creative release
From me to you
From me to you
Yeah, me to you

A common cliche' that's spoken today
says art imitates life
But life is an art form
that cannot be mastered

And once it's done,
art lives as a bastard

The bomber gives a final glance
but this time nothing's left to chance
Ultimate victory will be his
as he blows himself to bits

Here's my little masterpiece
A brand new creative release
From me to you
From me to you
Yeah, me to yo

(from *Game Show Teeth*)

Make It Snappy

Can a turtle jump a hurdle?
Purple Burt'll answer that
"Kurt can't jump one, but he'll bump one
out the way in minutes flat"

As you know I cannot go
much faster than a snail in snow
My legs are short and I support a big shell
Guess what? I'm slow!

Make it snappy
Make it snappy
I can hear you
It don't matter
Make it snappy
Make it snappy
I'm a turtle and that's that!

Snapping turtles are historic,
dinosauric, truth be told
So don't rush me, push or mush me
Have some respect for the old

You want speedy? Listen sweetie,
I would move it if I could
If what you pay for's to be safer
I am your guy - Understood?

I am sturdy, strong and trusty
You will get where you are headed
Don't expect to get there fast
'cause if you do you just don't get it

Make it snappy
Make it snappy
I can hear you
It don't matter

Make it snappy
Make it snappy
I'm a turtle and that's that!

(from *Purple Burt*)

Make Yourself at Home

Unwind
Take a load off your mind and recline
Make yourself at home

Get some rest
If you want, take a nap, be my guest
Make yourself at home

How do you get rid of the stress?
Show me how to get it off my chest
How do you ignore all the noise?
Tell me how to clear my head of the voice

Make yourself at home

Home isn't sweet and I don't wear hats
Quiet and peace don't even phone

Content
is the way you should feel laying there
You're meant to relax without even a care
Make yourself at home

Forget
that I'm sitting in the other room
Just let your mind go while I contemplate doom
Make yourself at home

How do you release all the pain?
Teach me how to open up the drain
How do you live with yourself?
Help me to retain my mental health

Make yourself at home
(Get me outta here)

(from *Game Show Teeth*)

Mesmerized

It's not my diet, it's perfectly balanced
All my vital electrons are valenced
More potent than a dose of extraordinary wisdom
There's something foreign in my system

Mesmerized
Hypnotized
I am walking around in a stupor
Spinning within a loop d' looper
Mesmerized

Mesmerized
Magnetized
I'm time-traveling in outer spatial
Rainbows unrolling below my facial
Mesmerized

This time it's love, oh this time it's love
Giddy inside, it's bonafide
I know this time it's love

Mesmerized
Google-eyed
All reality is out of phase now
Unclear again in a happy daze now
Mesmerized

This time it's love, oh this time it's love
Giddy inside, it's verified
I know this time it's love

Mesmerized

(from *FRED*)

Mr. Sir

Hey Mr. Sir
That toupee looks like rabbit fur
So long in the tooth
and still you think you're youthful
Mr. Sir
What's more important is interior
You'd be better off to hide that, to be truthful

Mr. Sir
Your wife is twenty years your junior
You should try to love her
while you're still active
Mr. Sir
You're the college girl's adulterer
It's a crime your daughter finds you unattractive

Hey Mr. Sir
Have a nice day, Mr. Sir
I mean go away, Mr. Sir!

Hey Mr. Sir
You're a fifty-year old teenager
who'll play spin the bottle
only once it's empty
Mr. Sir
Have you bribed your new tax auditor?
It's the only gamble you win consistently

Hey Mr. Sir
I wish you the best, Mr. Sir
But only in jest, Mr. Sir

You look real neato in a new tuxedo
but your bloated libido doesn't fit in a Speedo
You act so distinguished as if you were English
but the title you think you have was relinquished
long ago . . .

Hey Mr. Sir
You're a very wealthy barrister
who snatches all his cash from the poor and guilty
Mr. Sir
The perfect role model murderer
whose conscience was all gone
before the time of Uncle Milty

Hey Mr. Sir
So you're doing well, Mr. Sir?
Well then go to hell, Mr. Sir!

Hey Mr. Sir
Grrrrrrrrr!

(from *The Importance of Sauce*)

My Dumb Luck

Half a cup
just will not fill up
My dumb luck's no good

Horseshoe on the door
fell and hit the floor
Crushed my rabbit's foot

Won a lottery
stuck in bankruptcy
My misfortune's vast

Went and pinned the tail,
but the donkey bailed
What a sorry ass

Flip a coin, join the superstitious
Be resigned to what you find
'cause in time your dumb luck could turn
For that I burn

On top a ladder sat
my black hissing cat,
thirteen rungs above

It jumped and broke its fall,
cracking my mirror ball
when I gave it a shove

Ouija board says "What?"
Gives me paper cut
Now my palm is red

Floating leaves in tea
spell "You're kidding me"
Sympathy is dead

Throw the dice, twice the chance for trouble
Probability's aloof
and I know, my dumb luck is proof
May it go poof!

So when the dawn begins to break
will my dumb luck awaken?

And you may say that luck is tenuous
And you may say that luck is for the birds
And yet you try to earn the angels' fuss
I bet they never heard your praying

Survived a shipwreck
with fans of *Star Trek*
All of them were male

Found a diamond ring
stolen from a king
My reward was jail

That's the story of my dumb luck
Lest you think I am just some shmuck,
my dumb luck remains

(from *Game Show Teeth*)

My Second Record

Welcome to my second record
A new slew of tunes for you
Like the first one it is checkered
with a lot of words and food

My second, my second, my second record
This one took me quite awhile
You don't have to be all liquored
up for it to make you smile

Short and fast, slow and long
Here come all the other songs

(from *FRED*)

Neon Moon

Souvenir cheese! Souvenir cheese!
Meet the man himself!

Meteor burgers . . .
They're meatier

Warp-warp-gravitize
Brake, air-brake dancin'

"I'm grieving a crater-full of tears
Don't leave me on neon moon"

(from *pOp cOrn*)

New Kind of Human

Isn't it time for a new kind of human?
One so different they'll be assumin'
it could not be homosapien
No chance of ancestors ape-ian

One that doesn't need a god,
have a bod or lay down sod
One that will not shoot to kill,
take the pill or cook with dill
One that will not break from stress,
make a mess or stink at chess

Isn't it time for a new kind of human?
So if there are clouds mushroomin'
there'll be something 'round that's permanent
when we need a seed to germinate

For example, a sample member of this race
would have a blob of clay for faces
to mold into any form, so as not to have a norm
Next the neck would be a piston
to connect the clockwork system
which would run without a winding,
long as the piston is still binding to its source
Lemon juice of course
In the juice are nutrients pure and cured
to work in synchronistic timing
with the system's task assigning department
All throughout the juice solution
are the elements essential
for developments both mental and physical,
though it's done in a dish
You control it all fluidically,
though some would say that medically
it is not possible to have life without blood and brains

Isn't it time for a new kind of human?
One so different they'll be assumin'
it could not be homosapien
No chance of ancestors ape-ian

(from *HENWAY - Big Hair*)

New York Sunset

Lower Manhattan
Governor's Isle
Statue of Liberty
Red Hook for miles
Boats do a crisscross
Ferries roll by
Helicopters take off
Windows twinkle up high

If only I had this view
but the sliding vinyl room divider will have to do
Every night I miss this New York sunset
I feel like the sun is setting on me

Poked with so many needles
the pain becomes quaint
It would be a nice change
if one time I faint

Laying in bed,
watching TV
Getting my meals
through an IV
It's not uncommon,
but it is for me
All of you out there,
you've got my sympathy

If only I had this view
but the sliding vinyl room divider will have to do
Every night I miss this New York sunset
I feel like the sun is setting on me

Every day I don't get to see the world from my window,
shitty, shitty is the evening time
There's nothing about this in any way fine

Excited for UK,
end up in ER
CAT scans and colons
are no Trafalgar

Wearing a ragged hospital gown
Staring at biohazard warnings around
Reading a Kindle,
growing a beard
It is much more gray
than I had feared

If only I had this view
but the sliding vinyl room divider will have to do
Every night I miss this New York sunset
I feel like the sun is setting on me

(unrecorded)

Nine Mile Road

Meet me at the crux of the nine mile road,
on your feet of callouses
Come let us walk
'mongst the croaking of toads,
under clouds like palaces

Our love was lost but a long time ago
Poison words and circumstance
These days the cost is more than you know
to decline such fine romance

The nine mile road is our lifeline home
The nine mile road is a thorny rose
Until we laugh, until we grow
meet me at the nine mile road

Nine mile road,
bring us round again

(from *FRED*)

Nothing But a Soul

Pardon me, a part of me is reaching for release
The entire mass of me is asking for decrease

My left thumb said "See ya', chum"
and hit the road in hitchhike mode
The rest of my fingers chose not to linger
and took a turn at being a fern

Five pints of blood said "Later, bud!"
then fortified and oxidized some facial mud
A ribcage and a couple of bones
headed for the jungle as a xylophone

One week ago I was a whole
now I'm nothing but a soul

My brain went insane from the strain of pain
and took a plunge as a car wash sponge
Twenty-seven hairs that made up a curl
flocked to the locks of a newborn girl

Several organs and a gland
got a job as a billboard ampersand
An elbow turned to macaroni
My ponytail just joined a pony

One week ago I was a whole
now I'm nothing but a soul

When you pin a reincarnation
on the lapel of a flesh tuxedo,
anything that's left feels overdressed,
and "Let's split" becomes its common credo

Beauty marks, freckles, and some warts
became the imperfections in a piece of quartz

Some cartilage and a ligament
replaced the guard wires in an army tent

Testes and their penis bestie
made a foray to play croquet
The eyelids said "This is lame"
and turned into the shells in a shell game

One week ago I was a whole
now I'm nothing but a soul

(unrecorded)

Often I Saunter

In the rush, rush, rush of the day,
see the push and the crush of the people parade
Riding cars, bikes, buses and trains
through the Mach V circus of Ringmaster Fray
They've no time to clown

In the hush, hush, hush of the night,
near the plush of the pillow and the shush of polite
Fighting slapstick happenstance dreams
with a keystone 'copter cropping the scenes
It's time they slow down

So often I saunter
for want of a better way
Often I saunter about . . .

About 1 pm, adjoin to them a gent with a gradual gait
They buzz and blur but I prefer simply to perambulate
A slow-motion potentate

About 1 am, en route to REM
as masses and watches unwind
They snore and stir but next to her
I'm utterly calm and supine
An otter aloft in brine

It is such, such, such a short life
We are specs of dust in eternity's eyes
With so much, much, much far and wide,
watch us brush, brush, brush every detail aside
They don't see my frown

So often I saunter
for want of a better way
Often I saunter about . . .

(from *Game Show Teeth*)

Once

Oh, I'm the guy you'll only meet once in your life
I'm the guy you'll only meet once in your life
I'm the guy you'll only meet
I'm the guy you'll only meet
I'm the guy you'll only meet
You'll only meet me once

I opened the door for you at the place where you work
I sat next to you on our plane trip
I carried your bags at the hotel
I gave you the time of day

I'm the guy you'll only meet once in your life
I'm the guy you'll only meet once in your life
I'm the guy you'll only meet
I'm the guy you'll only meet
I'm the guy you'll only meet
You'll only meet me once

I'm the guy who checked you out
at the local meat market
I'm the guy who drove you home once,
for a small charge
I'm the guy who kissed you first

I'm the guy you dreamt about once in your life
One day I was responsible for all your children

I'm the guy you'll only meet once in your life
We'll only meet once

(from *pOp cOrn*)

One Billion Degrees Below

The wind don't blow
and there ain't no snow
at one billion degrees below

Nothing can live there
'cept a cold-blooded killer
at one billion degrees below

Hold your fingers, nose, and toes in
No matter, they'll be frozen
at one billion degrees below

You ain't just be chillin'
You be real bad illin'
at one billion degrees below

Don't need no degrees to know
it's not where you want to go

Little bitty icicles
ride on cool blue bicycles
at one billion degrees below

Too far from the origin
to be encouragin'
at one billion degrees below

Mr. Frost can't even bite
'cause his teeth chatter day and night
at one billion degrees below

Colder than the tail of a comet or
the lowest reading on the best thermometer
One billion degrees below

Don't need no degrees to know
it's not where you want to go

Shiver me timbers, I can't feel my limb-ers!

No bologna, olive loaf, or salami
No members of the Siberian army
at one billion degrees below

Hey Fahrenheit, Celsius, and Mr. Kelvin
I can look up and see a cold day in hell when
I'm one billion degrees below

Don't need no degrees to know
it's not where you want to go

(unrecorded)

One Side at a Time

Let's talk, just the two of us,
even though three of us are here
It's awkward for one of us
'cause one brain ain't enough for two ears

Tell it to me one side at a time
Otherwise I'm left right in the middle
Tell it to me one side at a time
I'm getting confused in stereo

Let's walk, just a few of us,
even though more of us are near
It's awkward for some of us,
for some of us don't listen, just hear

Tell it to me one side at a time
Otherwise I'm left right in the middle
Tell it to me one side at a time
I'm getting confused in stereo

When words come from two mouths
who can tell who mouths what?

Tell it to me one side at a time
otherwise I'm left right in the middle
Tell it to me one side at a time
I'm getting abused in stereo

High	Low
Yes	No
Stop	Go
Stop!	

Three's a crowd but two's a normal conversation

(from *pOp cOrn*)

Open

Open your eyes
Open your nose
Open your ears
Open your toes
Open your heart
Open your mind
Open your art
Open your find

But never be close-minded
unless you're buying clothes

Open your door
Open your book
Open your show
Open your soup
Open your lungs
Open your legs
Open your store
Open your eggs

But never close your bookstore
unless you go buy soup

See something?
Open it
See it open?
Ain't that something?
Open sea?
Fling something
Some see flings
as openings

Open your head
Open your pores
Open your shed
Open your shores

Open your home
Open your curls
Open your roof
Open your world

But never shear your head curls
unless you are a sheep

Open your tie
Open your cuffs
Open your coat
Open your stuff
Open your gift
Open your wings
Open your fist
Open your things

But never tie your wings back
except for fisticuffs

Open
You're open
and shut

(unrecorded)

Out of It

It's no joy to employ all of your senses all the time
To lose control of one or two would be just fine
In all my years, I can count on my fingers
the number of beers that hit me for a ringer

I wanna feel numb, act dumb, drink a drum of punch
Your thumb points down - You disapprove?
It's just a hunch

I'm gonna loosen up by juicin' up
This nervous knot has got to go
So here's a cup, please fill'er up
My level of tolerance is pretty low

The room is spinning
My eyesight's thinning
I am grinning
Because I'm out of it
and proud of it
I'm out of it

Sure a sharp mind is a valuable item
Got any distractions? I'd invite 'em

My legs are rubbery
My stomach's blubbery
Where is the shrubbery?
Because I'm out of it
No doubt of it
I'm out of it

I'll harass you, then embarrass you
but only because I'm crocked
With a reputation wrecked and a close relation decked
I should be docked

I'm stumbling,
a bumbling fool
You're grumbling
Give me that stool
Because I'm out of it
Not proud of it
I'm out of it
But no more!

Won't you lead me to the door?

(unrecorded)

Pip Squeak

Pip squeak (you are a)
Pip squeak
A little oinky pig-face pip squeak
(You are) so weak
(Yes you are) so weak
What a little sniveling geek
(You are) so meek
(Yes you are) so meek
A little oinky pig-face pip squeak

(from *pOp cOrn*)

Pluto

All aboard, all aboard for Pluto
Got my skis and my deep-freeze suit-o
We will fly as fast as light
Got to get there by tonight
See us soar as we head for Pluto

Gonna land, gonna land on Pluto
On the sand, use a parachute-o
Snowy peaks fill the horizon
and they sure look appetizin'
Flew so far, here we are on Pluto

Push off, slide down
Speed up, glide 'round
Aloft, back flip
Hit soft, then slip
Become snowball
Best day of all!

This is plutopia!
This is plutopia!!
This is plutopia!!!
My secret ski-slopia!!!!

If I lived, if I lived on Pluto
I'd sell hot cocoa and make lots of loot-o
Then I'd build a jetpack playground
Kids would fill it with their "Yay!" sounds
What a time, glad that I'm on Pluto

Was it fun, was it fun on Pluto?
Never have I had such a hoot-o
Can a dream come true? Well can it?
Look no further than this planet
Got to be, got to ski on Pluto

(from *Purple Burt*)

President

Political correctness has never been my forte'
I can't pass a singles bar
without debating who'll be naughty

Let me kiss your big red lips,
my favorite oval orifice
I must concede they leave me speechless

If you second all my terms
and I can count on your support
Get set for some supreme courting

At this dress-to-impress conference
there's no question you're my answer
I'm your romancer in chief

In your interpersonal politics
I want to be your President

I'll erect a monument to our love
if we have our inaugural ball
I'd gladly stuff your ballot box
Take a look at this push poll

With a declaration of dependence
our congress is my solemn duty
I'd never have the constitution
to veto such a cutie

If this first pitch I'm throwing out
is a win for diplomacy
I'll phone you up on live TV
to praise you for choosing me

I nominate you to be my longest running mate
Wipe your weeping water gates
You're my vice, I'm your candid date

In your interpersonal politics
I want to be your President

I don't mean to be a campaign in the ask
but what's the state of our union?
You're not my first lady, but you could to be my last

With your dad's approval rating
as a ringing endorsement
I vote for a swearing in with many happy returns

Let's hold a secret service with a few select constituents
We'll live in a big white house,
complete with brand new cabinets

I've got capital to spend on you
This party's too conservative so
reach across the aisle,
grab my glad hand and let's go

In your interpersonal politics
I want to be your President
I can mend that ever-present dent in your heart

(unrecorded)

Pretty Pretty New York City

England's immature
They still think Benny Hill is funny
France we all deplore
They talk in French, their cheese is runny
L.A. is too chic
"Earthquakes shake the best martinis"
Men in Rome will gladly take you home
to show you their zucchinis

Why not visit pretty pretty New York City?
So exquisite,
even garbage men are witty
What time is it?
It's time for you to go!

Taxis are a trip up and downtown in a jiffy
Each of them equipped
with toiletries to keep you spiffy
Subways are serene
Wine and dine with perfect strangers
Repartee' and creme brulee
Hey! Gaining weight is your only danger

Why not visit pretty pretty New York City?
Please don't miss it
Just a week and you'll be giddy
What time is it?
It's time for you to go!

Walk along the avenue
Meet and greet ten million friendly faces
Bow and curtsy,
say 'How'd you do?"
Grinning puts a winning face
on all human races
It's the bestest of places!

Climb the Empire State
Lady Liberty's your escort
Perfume fills the air
from Central Park to South Street Seaport
Children love Times Square
A cornucopia of kooky
Young and old, grab your coat
Write that note, it's time to play hooky

C'mon visit pretty pretty New York City
How explicit
need we be singing this ditty?
What time is it?
It's time for us to go!

(from *FRED*)

Previously Unreleased

There's something in my past you never knew about
I kept it to myself but secretly I'm proud
It might complete the picture or help fill in the gaps
of what appeared to merely be a momentary lapse

It didn't fit with all the rest of who I was
Nonetheless, this current mess
could use a dose of what it does

This quiet guy was once a beast . . .
Previously Unreleased
This slender gent knew how to feast . . .
Previously Unreleased

I've tried to be the best at everything I've done
but sometimes it ain't bad to have comparison
My repertoire is farther-reaching than you think
Tastefulness can exist with the kitchen sink

I can't pawn myself off as something that I'm not
My checkered past will surely trash
the goodwill that I think I've got

This grounded guy was an artiste . . .
Previously Unreleased
Still losing hair I had increased . . .
Previously Unreleased

Unpredictability is on my calling card
It's the best excuse for me
if I sang twangy bluegrass in a DayGlo unitard

My obligation is contractual to you,
yet I might fill it with some silly indiscretions,
so please don't sue?

This atheist felt like a priest . . .
Previously Unreleased
Now smooth as silk but once so creased . . .
Previously Unreleased
This joker used to be so triste . . .
Previously Unreleased
I'm on the rise but once sought yeast . . .
Previously Unreleased

(from *SING SING*)

Purple Burt

Purple Burt eats green beans,
orange porridge and red bread
Purple Burt drinks blue juice,
wears pink mink and black slacks
Purple Burt smokes hope dope
His brain is a kaleidoscope
Purple Burt is color blind, Purple Burt's invisible
I'm Purple Burt, you're Purple Burt,
I'm . . .

Purple Burt rides the side of a rainbow
He's got one-zillion color TVs
Purple Burt dreams of skiing Pluto
as he naps in a prism tree
Purple Burt stays alert by eating lots of purple dirt
Purple Burt is color blind, Purple Burt's invisible
I'm Purple Burt, you're Purple Burt

Purple Burt has a brother, Purple Herbert
Herbert lives in a tin of herbal sherbet
He spends his days slurping and burping

Purple Burt drives to work
on his snapping turtle named Kurt
He keeps gasses sealed in glasses
All of these are inert
Purple Burt can't exert
His little purple heart is hurt
Purple Burt is color blind, Purple Burt's invisible
I'm Purple Burt, you're Purple Burt

(from *The Importance of Sauce* and *Purple Burt*)

Reach By Speech

Don't put us to sleep when you're at the wheel
You can't expect us to feel
either way when you talk
Indelible ink's not made of chalk

You make your marks with blunted points
Tongues are not immovable joints
We could swing either way,
but only if we're pushed today

Reach by speech
Each word counts
You won't catch prey
if you don't pounce

To influence you must impress us
Boredom only will depress thus
don't go fishing - Why not wait?
Your hooks don't hold your soggy bait

Reach by speech
Each word counts
You won't catch prey
if you don't pounce

Every year it's someone new
but those tricks, they're always old
How can one choose a quality speaker
when there's no volume control?

Reach by speech
Each word counts
You won't wake me
with muffled sounds

(from *pOp cOrn*)

Ribbons & Bows

Ribbons & bows, ribbons & bows
My baby goes for ribbons & bows
My baby goes for ribbons & bows quicker than roses

How was your day? Oh that's just great
Now will you listen to me, dear?

As long as I bring home a box
that holds something expensive,
for you it's immaterial
that my anger is so extensive

Ribbons & bows, ribbons & bows
My baby goes for ribbons & bows quicker than roses

Presently your present sits so pleasantly alone
Wining when we're dining
will not make that gift your own
I know that you're adorable and my career is famous
You know we are wrapped up in something
that cannot contain us
You see I see that all you see in me
are gifts and paparazzi
But what you get is what I see
as something that will never stop me
thinking about ringing your stinking little neck
with some of those

Ribbons & bows, ribbons & bows
My baby goes for ribbons & bows
My baby goes for ribbons & bows quicker than roses
Ribbons & bows, ribbons & bows
My baby knows what money can buy

(from *pOp cOrn*)

Runaway Train of Thought

Hey, I've got a bright idea . . .
Drive and drink a case of beer
Take a long walk off a short pier
We'll beat her up, no one will hear
Who cares about the atmosphere?
Let's humiliate a queer
Snort some meth and go shoot deer
Steroids help my sports career

Watch the logic disappear
as attitudes get cavalier
Something's locked the mental gear
This head of steam could quickly veer
Go hide until the coast is clear!

Runaway train of thought
With emotion at the helm
of a locomotive cerebellum
Runaway train of thought

(unrecorded)

She Was Soooooooooooooo Hot!

She was sooooooooooooo hot!

Her eyes would fry you
So svelte she'd melt you
Even under drizzle she would sizzle
Anything she handed you branded you

1-2-3-4-5
She was sooooooooooooo hot!

My lips would blister when I kissed her
My arms would smolder when I'd hold her

You know she was comin' 'cause
a cake would bake,
a stew would stew,
oil would boil,
and batter would spatter

2-3-4

Where she lays down would slowly brown
Only way to distinguish her is with an extinguisher
With a glass of wine she would flambe'
Move in close, we'll both saute'

Cold hard cash would turn to ash
Ice cream would turn to steam

1-2-3-4-5-6-7-8-9-10-11-12-13-14-15
She was sooooooooooooo hot!

(from *HENWAY - Big Hair*)

She's Dynamite!

Check out that chick over there
Electric eyes and fiery hair
When our lips meet we'll both ignite
Shaboom shaboom
She's dynamite!

She's the juice that's in my wire
We're the match that starts a fire
Tigress tigress burning bright
Shaboom shaboom
She's dynamite!

There's no question who's in charge
See my private salute her Sarge
She'll blow your mind to smithereens
once you pump her gasoline

My Bic
Her wick
One hard flick and tick tock tick, yeah!

What a blast it would be
to tap some of her energy
mc^2 = she
One hot piece of TNT

C'mon babe and drop that bomb
Send us both to Kingdom Come
The heat you make is hot and white
Shaboom shaboom
She's dynamite!

We'll explode as one tonight
Shaboom shaboom
She's dynamite!

(from *Game Show Teeth*)

Shedding One's Tread

Miles and miles of smiles and tears
Many years, many fears
Now it's time to shift gears

Worked on ethic, pride and need
Enough to feed a family
We'd never tolerate any greed

Two-thirds a hundred and changing again
Life can drive one to think
of that youthful fountain as the sink
that's soaking the man that has been

Shedding one's tread, shedding one's tread
Entirely up to me
Shedding one's tread, shedding one's tread
Retirement

I used to have a grip on life
My work worked as a sturdy tread
But now I sit home with my wife
My tire's bald as is my head

Shedding one's tread, shedding one's tread
Entirely up to me
Shedding one's tread, shedding one's tread
Retirement

(from *pOp cOrn*)

Simplification

Thoughts are fighting for their way
so much more than they ought today
atop a train that's runaway,
increasing in it's speed
I watch the rhythm of the land
as it flies by I understand
that hills and trees and rivers grand
have everything I need

Experimental convolution's
ruining my constitution
Too much fatty food for thought
is poisoning the feed
Like Newton did in days gone by,
ideas an apple in his eye,
he cut right to the core
and needed nothing but a seed

This thinking better cease
Give me a little peace

Simplification
My motivation

Take a trip to England
to a place that's older than dirt
Beauty that's spine tinglin'
Finally finding a loss for words

Cast aside all luxury
The only thing deluxe should be
a setting for the ideas
that you're getting in your mind
Take the ones you want to use,
throw them in a centrifuge
Spin it and when finished,
open up and you will find

My brain is in a whirl
I'm searching for that pearl

Simplification
Mental vacation

(from *The Importance of Sauce*)

Sing Anyway

Tunes are made to play and to be sung
To take either away
would be killing half the fun
You should not get embarrassed or feel shy
Even those with laryngitis
should give it a try

Imagine if you had a name like mine?
People would expect you
to be singing all the time
So even if you have a so-so voice,
whether to or whether not
is hardly any choice

Sing anyway

Don't let them tell you not to
Take it from me you've got to
open your mouth up wide
Show us with all your pride
No I don't mean your tonsils
Belt out a song and once you
get over how you sound,
everybody will gather 'round

Opera, soul and pop are here for you
There's disco, gospel, punk 'n rap,
plus rock and country too
But even if you just try "Doe a Deer,"
the worst thing that can happen
is we cover up our ears

Sing anyway

(from *Purple Burt*)

666-Luck

Are you looking for luck?
Don't go away
Today is now your luck day
Leave your name and number
and the best time for us to call,
and then you'll be lucky once and for all

(from *pOp cOrn*)

Sleepless

Sleepless, oh baby I'm sleepless
I can't count sheep when I cannot count on you
lying in the same bed
Sleepless, oh you keep me sleepless
Not a wink, not a drink at all

You worry about me so much
that I make you move in your sleep
enough to give me motion sickness
Still somehow I'm able to keep you
and you keep me too,
sleepless

I owe you girl for caring a lot,
but I'm gonna sleep in a cot
Sleeping with you in the same bed
is going to my head
You're stirring in bed
and stirring my head over you,
and all the things you're dreaming,
sleepless

Oh honey, the sun is out
Isn't it time for your breakfast-time pout?
All because I'm sleepless

I'm overly tired of my wife
a very large part of my life
Driving me to a groggy grave
being bedridden with her

(from *pOp cOrn*)

Sleeptown

Bring it down, now

The "lay flat" light is lit, please recline
as we carve a tunnel through an arc
of jumping sheep clouds
We'll snack on pills and warm milk
We'll snack on pills and warm milk
Don't forget the pillow headset

Bring it down, bring it down

White noise paints night
Dull descends like mighty nightgowns
In the aisles, on the wings
Everything, dull

Bring it down, bring it down

Our dream feature for this evening
stars a cast of thousands from your life
Set in surroundings of a logic jumbled,
all seen while you toss and tumble

Sex with stars, fights, flights
Endless home runs, endless runs home
Giants, gnomes
Murder, birth, sadness, mirth, space, Earth
Fall from a cliff, make a song, time travel

Slight delay, can't sight a runway
There's congestion, circle 'round
Soon we'll land in Sleeptown

Peer past prop propellers
cutting puffy parallels to peek through

See Sneaky Pete The Peep Clown
prancing, dancing, chancing sound
through the streets of Sleeptown

Check out the second-hand clicking rhythm
marching metronome corps
winding on to chime time

Bring it down, bring it down
About to land in Sleeptown

The Eyelid Kids have started a movement,
pacing, pouncing back and forth 'cross clouded ground
They cruise in snooze to snore store
to rev their nose and throat motors

That quiet wining, pitter-patter
of a cat or dog may shatter calm
Armed, the squad of cotton wad rushes to the rescue!

A busker croons a womb tune over a heartbeat
far away down Dusky Street

Sleeptown, sleep

(from *HENWAY - Big Hair*)

Slow Down Now

Leaky faucets drip drip
Scissors going snip snip
Clocks and watches tick tock
Kiddies jumping hopscotch

Rockers chopping axe licks
Actress smacks her lipstick
Ponies prancing clip clop
Chickies hatching egg tops

Dialers dialing touch-tone
Doggies dig for big bones
Critics ripping film clips
Brokers phoning stock tips

Stop stop the chop chop
Everything rush much too much
Stop stop the chop chop
No one's yelling "Mush! Mush!"
S L O W   D O W N   N O W

Rappers rappin' hip hop
Acrobats do flip-flops
Gasmen testing dipsticks
Goalies doing dropkicks

Radar readouts blip blip
Veggies dredging clam dips
Frat boys cracking flip tops
Parents snapping snap shots

Bitchy sisters nitpick
Summer lovers picnic
Mommies mailing box tops
Catchers snatching pop ups

Stop stop the chop chop
Everything rush much too much
Stop stop the chop chop
No one's yelling "Mush! Mush!"
S L O W   D O W N   N O W

Act/react/act/act/react
Act/act/react/react/act/act
Act/react/react/act/act
Act/act/react/act/act/act
Act/react/smack/act/react
Smack/act/react/react/attack!

Tablets plop plop fizz fizz
Teenage jackers jizz jizz
Smokers crushing cig butts
Diesel engines chug chug

Jive mofos high five
Bees swarming their hive
Herders rounding up sheep
Horns honking beep beep

Movie makers clap sticks
Smokers flicking their Bics
Beefheart Captain click clacks
Grannies canning nik-naks

Filibusters talk talk
Doorbell ringers ding dong
Insect kingdoms buzz buzz
Leaden headaches throb throb

Stop stop the chop chop!

(unrecorded)

Smile Awhile

My brother burps,
I'm invisible and my girlfriend's away
My turtle's slow,
I'm still colorblind and I eat dirt all day
Even though I am sad, I know how to be glad
I take my frown and turn it around
with a brand new game that I play

Smile awhile,
and laugh too
Smile awhile,
you have to
think of something funny then
tell the funny thing to all your friends
They will pass the funny thing around
Soon the only thing you'll hear
is a happy sound
Smile awhile
It's an easy thing to do!

You can't be sad with a silly grin
and a gleam in your eyes
So jump around, be a clown
and you'll only see sunny skies
You will always have fun
with chuckling by the ton
as long as you remember to
keep your mind on the happiness prize

Smile awhile,
and giggle
Smile awhile,
be tickled
Smile awhile,
and laugh too
Smile awhile,
you have to

think of something funny then
tell the funny thing to all your friends
They will pass the funny thing around
Soon the only thing you'll hear
is a happy sound

Smile awhile
It's the only thing to do!

(from *Purple Burt*)

Splendid

Why do I wile my day away sad and glum?
Why do I hide my smile away cold and numb?
As the light slowly slides away there's relief
Time is nigh for my bow tie and cane
Game show teeth so . . .

I hop in a taxi
and sit in the back seat
Looking all snazzy and sipping champagne
I'm newly contented
'cause I'm feeling splendid

So call me Mr. Night Life
but please don't say it 'round my wife
Ain't got time for high strife
Sing and dance and be gay
Keep the daylight away

Maybe it's the way that I wear my hat
Or maybe it's the "scooby-doos" in my scat
Fact of the matter is I'm all that!

I'm charming and dapper
And what is the capper,
a talented tapper with style and grace
I'm highly befriended
now I'm feeling splendid
(That is why my frown has upended)

So call me Mr. Night Life
but please don't say it 'round my wife
Ain't got time for high strife
Sing and dance and be gay
Keep the daylight away

(from *FRED*)

Spring (Is Waiting For a Chance To) Spring

Something in the air says the winter's ending
People start to come outside looking for some friending
Daylight's saving up extra time to do its thing
Spring is waiting for a chance to spring

Seeds are getting set now the snow is melting
Baseball batters swing, hoping for some belting
Buds are popping up, lovers get set for a fling
Spring is waiting for a chance to spring

The sun is trying but the clouds won't let it
If trees could make a breeze
you bet those clouds would regret it

Heavy coats are gone, girls show off their legging
Birds are starting to chirp now as they do their egging
Bees can hardly wait to find someone they can sting
Spring is waiting for a chance to spring

Bears are waking up from their hibernating
Fishermen can't wait to begin their baiting
Ice cream trucks tune up, practicing their ding-a-ling
Spring is waiting for a chance
Break out your short sleeves and pants
Spring is waiting for a chance to spring

(from *SING SING*)

Steal This

Go ahead and steal this
I'd be happy if you do
You must know someone who'd want a few of these
Just to see it was forbidden
Now it isn't even hidden
Steal this, I'm begging you
Pretty please?

Many things are not worth keeping
Once they're gone there'll be no weeping
To make some space for what is needed
a jungle of junk should be weeded
out you go, old Mr. Useless
A rug that's bald, a comb that's toothless

Go ahead and steal this
I double dare you
The prospect of prospective trouble
shouldn't scare you

I bet you too were once bereft
of pride until some petty theft
developed into big-time robbery
A kind of low-life high-crime snobbery

One man's honest, one's criminal
The choice's voice is all subliminal
A conscious conscience makes a meter
for the mind to tip and teeter
back and forth, south or north
Both poles can be cold of course

Go ahead and steal this
Take what you want, I won't look
Hope I can tell what you took

(unrecorded)

Summer Morning, I'm Due

Conversation, we lit up
with the grass on our backs and minds
Between my spring and my fall
we turned and learned what we would find

Summer morning, I'm due and melted away
Summer morning, I'm due and melted away from you

My shoulders are colder
It'd be a breeze to leave
But all my falls are back to you
Your warmth meant much to me

Those feelings, they fade like my tan
And like dew on top of green,
those minutes which just dripped off the hour
will not last longer than how long they can be seen
on this

Summer morning, I'm due and melted away
Summer morning, I'm due to fall out of love with you

(from *pOp cOrn*)

Superstar Maker To The Stars

You're gonna be big
You're gonna be huge
You're gonna be tops
You're gonna be gigantic

Just stick with me kid
You'll be on the news
You're gonna make bucks
It's gonna be fantastic

I got a good hunch
we're gonna do lunch
You, me and a bunch
of those top bigwigs

We cannot go wrong
I'll shmooze 'em along
and play them your song
I bet we net you six figs

Because . . .
I am the Superstar Maker to the Stars
I will bring you fame,
or if you're a star, then super-fame
I am the Superstar Maker to the Stars
Superstar making's my game
and Morty Moneyman's my name

Hey kid, I don't mean to be a pest
but I'm a stickler for particulars
That said, for you to be your best
you gotta cut those school extracurriculars

This thing is a smash
Start counting your cash
Just watch 'em all dash
to the record store

With me by your side
we'll travel worldwide
Get ready to hide
when fans yell more, more, more!

I am the Superstar Maker to the Stars
I will bring you fame,
or if you're a star, then super-fame
I am the Superstar Maker to the Stars
Superstar making's my game
and Morty Moneyman's my name

(from *Purple Burt*)

Swingin'

Shoulda been a doctor
Coulda been a lawyer
Now I'm up in this sequoia
Gonna cash a paycheck
with my neck by swingin'
(What am I thinkin'?)

Shoulda saved my money
Coulda had a cushion
The economy is Bush-in'
Ain't got squat hid in my cot
I'm swingin'
(Ouch, this is stingin')

Swingin' . . . Over debt
Swingin' . . . With no net
Swingin' . . . You can bet
a tax cut ain't no tourniquet

Woulda had a chance
to pick a new profession
but thanks to this damn recession
my only skill is sippin' swill
I'm swingin'
(My phone isn't ringin')

Swingin' . . . With no bat
Swingin' . . . I'm no cat
Swingin' . . . This habitat
ain't got scraps to feed a rat

I can't afford the water bill
to even stay afloat
The only good noose that I got
is tight around my throat

Shoulda been a doctor
Coulda been a lawyer
Now I can't find no employer
that'll pay a dime for killing time
by swingin' (I'm finished singin')

(from *FRED*)

Swinging On The Family Tree

It's Saturday afternoon,
one o'clock, Granny's house
Grandpapa says Aunt Sarah's
bringing her brand new spouse
Uncle Mel, who the hell is he?
Well he'll miss out if he comes late
'cause picking apples from the apple tree
and filling up a wooden crate
has easily got to be,
altogether, really fun with your family

Did anyone ever tell you that
you've got your daddy's brains,
you've got your mommy's looks?
But I can't seem to pinpoint your personality
Swinging on the family tree
Swinging on the family tree
Swinging on the family tree
Swinging   on

Cousins and nephews, some twice removed
Aunties and uncles, some act removed
Granny and Grandpa are very confused
not which is which but just who is who

You've got your daddy's thoughts,
you've got your mommy's smirks
Swinging on the family tree
Swinging on the family tree
Swinging on the family tree
Swinging   on

The cool little breeze, these marvelous trees
It's almost a state of sweet utter bliss
But drinking my family's sharp apple cider
is getting me mentally utterly pissed

Swinging on the family tree
Swinging on the family tree
Swinging on the family tree
Swinging

(from *pOp cOrn*)

The Last Nice Day

On the last nice day it was smooth sailing
The sky was bright
The breeze was light
The sun was just right

On the last nice day not a soul was ailing
The air was clear
There was ample beer
We were happy to be here

The last nice day was a humdinger
The last nice day was one for the books
The last nice day was a bell ringer
The last nice day earned a "Gadzooks!"

Will the last nice day be the last nice day?
It depends on what your definition of nice is
Some are only happy when everyone else is in crisis

The last nice day was hunky dory
The last nice day was a real beaut
The last nice day made some history
The last nice day made every other nice day moot

On the last nice day,
far away, the storm was forming . . .

(from *SING SING*)

The Man That Talked Too Much

Always rehearsing the art of conversing
by rapidly dispersing words

The man that talked too much
had a diction addiction
which clouded his nouns
and verbs with verbiage
even unclear to Shakespearian heritage

The man that talked too much

The man that talked too much
could not hear himself thinking
His dabble in gab'll assist you in Scrabble
but you'll never topple his tower of babble

The man that talked too much

The man that talked too much
met the woman that never listened
The man that talked too much was speechless
He was speechless
He was speechless

The man that talked too much
asked the woman for some kissing
The man that talked too much was smitten
but she bit him
He was smitten
but she spit him out

The man that talked too much
preferred violence to silence
A harangue of slang, insults and sarcasm
jumped from his tongue
in a bungeeing spasm

The man that talked too much was
taught that if you speak like dictionary leak
it is a fine technique for showing he's a geek
and he'd be better off if he just shut his beak

(from *Game Show Teeth*)

The Mitch & Jude Show

Hey there, we're Mitch and Jude
One hip chick and bitchin' dude
If you need to unhitch your mood . . .
We can do it!

Hi there, we're Mitch and Jude
With tasty tunes like kitchen food
If you want songs so rich and good . . .
We can do it!

Ho there, we're Mitch and Jude
Opposite the niche of rude
Wanna scratch your itch for cute?
We can do it!

We'll "sha-la-la" and "oo-ee-oo"
until the sun goes down or up
So why don't you "tra-la-la" and do it too?
Let's turn all the world's "uh-uhs"
into one big "Yup!"

Hey there, we're Mitch and Jude
We can do it!

(rough demo)

The Pageant Song

Everybody put your hands together
Everybody put your hands together
Everybody put your hands together now!

You've reached the top, the top of the ladder
You've never stopped and we couldn't be gladder
You're the people's choice tonight!

For one whole year, the world has your name on it
Do anything you want to do
You're A#1 tonight, oooooh!

You're the highfalutin, rootin' tootin' top banana
You've passed all the rest, you've mastered the test
You're the cream of the crop,
you're the absolute best!

You're the picture of perfection
with an element of style
Noteworthy disposition
and that old familiar smile

With a superhuman effort of which we now speak
you've climbed the highest mountain
and reached it's snowy
peak peak peak peak peak peak PEAK!

Alabama Alaska Arizona Arkansas California
Colorado Connecticut Delaware District of Columbia
Florida Georgia Hawaii Idaho Illinois Indiana
Iowa Kansas Kentucky Louisiana Maine Maryland
Massachusetts Michigan Mississippi Missouri
Minnesota Montana Nebraska Nevada New Hampshire
New Jersey New Mexico New York North Carolina
North Dakota Ohio Oklahoma Oregon Pennsylvania
Rhode Island South Carolina South Dakota Tennessee

Texas Utah Vermont Virginia Washington West Virginia
Wisconsin Wyoming

The courage of a Dr. Martin Luther King
"I have a dream"
The grace and style of a Fred Astaire
"Go Fred go!"
The goal-scoring prowess of a Rod Gilbert
"Gilbert shoots, he scores!"
With a little Tricky Dicky thrown in

The moment is here
The time is near
The answer is clear to me
It's you, you, you, you,
you, you, you, you,
you, you, you, YOU!

(from *HENWAY - Big Hair*)

The Popcorn Tree

Let's neck near a nook in the storybook
of the popcorn tree
We'll nap near a knot, once a lookout spot
to protect Club Glee

There's a kernel of truth of a fountain of youth
at the popcorn tree
So come lay on the ground with a crunching sound
for infinity

Popcorn tree
Me and thee
Popcorn tree
Ecstasy

What more can I do to butter you up?

The wee kernels grow
and in spring finally show their presence
On the hottest day near the end of May
they pop into pleasance

The grass turns from green to fluffy yellow
Can there be any greater sight or smello?

Let's bunk near the trunk 'til we're sugar-drunk
at the popcorn tree
We'll laze on the maize in a happy haze-filled recipe

Popcorn tree
Me and thee
Popcorn tree
Ecstasy

What more can I do to butter you up?

(unrecorded)

This Fitting Room

They've been following the same pattern for years
like it's one of the old styles
He's hemmed in to the point of tears
"Too loose around the crotch?" she smiles
"Try this on for size!" he sneers
In this fitting room

They could never find a way to stitch things up
and clashed like polka dots and plaid
"I hate your fits!" he brings up
"The alterations you just had
will never make me stop!"
she said with evil gloom

In this fitting room they bickered for years
where casual seemed quite formal
It's funny how people so clothes-minded
could live through a marriage so normal

It's only fitting that the full-length mirror
would reflect the value of his dollar
But who would imagine a wife in high fashion
and a husband with black shirt and white collar?

In this fitting room they bickered for years
where casual seemed quite formal
It's funny how people so clothes-minded
could live through a marriage so normal

This fitting room, this fitting room
Not fit for proper love
The musty air that lurked in there
could suffocate a dove

(unrecorded)

This Friend

I have this friend who's going through tough times lately
and he feels really alone
I recommend his chances would improve greatly
if he'd just answer the phone

If I were him, and thank god I'm not, but if I were
I would go to a shrink
In the interim, on his behalf I am counting
on you to say what you think

He could use your advice, he could use it
He could use your advice or he may lose it

He's in a rut and I tell you what he needs
is a whole new life to embrace
But in my gut I'd be too afraid to change
if I put myself in his place

He could use your advice, he could use it
He'd improve with your advice so he'll refuse it

When you know someone as well as you know yourself
you can't help feel their pain
So you hope some sympathy is a show of help
but helplessness remains

This is the last verse and I can tell you
me and my friend are starting to sweat
If you need more time to ponder our situation
I'll make this a novelette

We could use your advice, we could use it
We could use your advice or we may lose it

(from *The Importance of Sauce*)

This Is a Song

This is a song
and this is a verse
There will be three
This one is first
Story begins
and melody grows
Leading into
the part we all know

This is the chorus
This is the chorus
This is the chorus
You see how it repeats
This is the chorus
This is the chorus
This is the chorus
And now we will proceed to

Verse number two
Similar yes
The melody stays
but lyrics progress
That added guitar
is something to do
to get you worked up
as we head into

Another chorus
Another chorus
Another chorus
Pretty much the same
Another chorus
Another chorus
And now before us
we have the middle eight

This is the part of the song
where the meaning
is often spelled out in a literal fashion
to clarify anything poetic
or that was hinted at up to this point
Since it will only last for eight bars
which is a short time compared to
the previous sections
feel free to continue
to ruminate further
as we now move on to a solo

Verse number three
Familiar old friend
Summing things up
so near to the end
Everything left
that needs to be said
is nothing compared
to what lies ahead

The final chorus
The final chorus
The final chorus
Sung with lots of strength
The final chorus
The final chorus
The final chorus
is also twice the length
The final chorus (with extra words)
The final chorus (with extra words)
The final chorus (with extra words)
that blend together here
The final chorus (five seconds left)
The final chorus (four seconds left)
The final chorus (three seconds left)
before we disappear

(from *Game Show Teeth*)

Thrash Dash

1-2-3-4
Punk junk flunk drunk
gunk spunk dunk stunk
bunk sunk hunk skunk
1-2-3-4
Smash trash crash bash
slash mash clash gash
brash lash stash ash
1-2-3-4
Punk dash stunk flash
trunk ash hunk hash
funk thrash shrunk cash
1-2-3
Aaaaaaaaaaaaaaaaaaaaaaaaaahhhhhhhhhhhhhhhhh!
1-2-3
Aaaaaaaaaaaaaaaaaaaaaaaaaahhhhhhhhhhhhhhhhh!
1-2-3
Aaaaaaaaaaaaaaaaaaaaaaaaaahhhhhhhhhhhhhhhhh!
1-2-3-4
Punk punk punk punk
punk punk punk punk
punk punk

(from *EXTRAVAGANZA DELUXE!*)

To Be There For You

You can't catch a cab when it rains in New York
And you can't get a two-month old infant to walk
And you can't drink the wine before you pop the cork
But you can count on me to be there for you
You can count on me to be there for you

You can't read a book if you sit in the dark
And you can't climb a tree if you don't grab the bark
And you can't yell "Who goes there!"
without shouting "Hark!"
But you can count on me to be there for you
You can count on me to be there for you

Reliable
I'm so reliable
I'm liable
to be quite desirable
I dare you to find a viable
alternative to me and you

You can't raise your voice if you don't have a tongue
And you can't be too old if you've never been young
And you can't be a porn star if you're not well hung
But you can count on me to be there for you
You can count on me to be there for you

Reliable
I'm so reliable
I'm liable
to be quite desirable
I'll swear on a pile of bibles,
anything you wish is my command

It's easy to dream up
a way for us to team up
Just fade the love theme up
and follow my script

A train has no end if there is no caboose
And you can't squeeze a fruit without producing juice
A gang cannot hang you unless there's a noose
But you can count on me to be there for you
You can count on me to be there for you

(from *The Importance of Sauce*)

Today Night

Ooh hoo hoo hoo, we do love
Together
Today night!

I see you dancing at the disco
D - I - S - C - O
The thing in my pants, he really go go go
G – O
G - O - G - O

Ooh hoo hoo hoo, we do love
Together
Today night!

American hair, American eyes
American head, American ankle
American mouth, American thigh
I want American my!

Ooh hoo hoo hoo, we do love
Together
Today night!

Girl, I'm a guy
Girl, I'm a guy
Girl, I'm a guy
Girl, I'm a guy!

Ooh hoo hoo hoo, we do love
Together
Today night!
Ooh hoo hoo hoo, we do love
Forever
Today night!

(from *The Importance of Sauce*)

Treasure

Anchors aweigh
out in the spray
Treasure awaits
sealing our fate

Wait 'til the bounty's found
We'll hear the trumpets sound
And we will all drink down our beer

Ocean of gray
No land in sight
Caps on the waves
for twenty nights
Winds starts to play
Sails are fastened tight

What if we run aground?
What if the ship's unsound?
What if we all just drown in fear?

Gold . . . Look at the rainbow
Gold . . . Look at the sunset

What if the world is round?
What if we fail the crown?
What if we sail around for years?

(from *FRED*)

Tribute Band

What goes around comes around . . .

Back in '76 I had a hit
I went on the TV and sang it a bit
Just as fast, I fell out of favor
In a drunken rage allegedly I shot my neighbor

I faked my own death and grew a goatee
Then I flew the coop using the alias "Guy"
I settled in Belgium and turned a new page
'til some karaoke got me back on the stage

I did my old hit kind of rusty
and some folks came up for a word
They said
"We are a group that covers his stuff
and you're the closest to the real thing
we've ever heard!"

Now I'm in a tribute band to myself,
singing as me being somebody else
In a tribute band to myself

My back catalogue was becoming a slog
so I wrote us some new stuff in the style of prog
I gotta be careful not to blow my own cover
That's why I changed our band name
to an anagram of my Swedish lover

A year passed by, then my luck ran out
The authorities nabbed me
right in the middle of "Shout!"
The press had a field day
My sentence was long
There's no singing in Sing Sing
and that's including this song

Behind The Music glossed right over my discography
It's okay
Now I'm making multi-millions
with an autobiography

Thanks to being in a tribute band to myself,
singing as me being somebody else
In a tribute band to myself

What goes around comes around . . .

(from *SING SING*)

Trick-Knee Trixie

Narrator: In the car, to the bar . . .
Wife: What a night ahead!
Narrator: At the bar . . .
Bouncer: Sorry sir, it's ten bucks a head
Husband: Why so much?
Wife: Why we just want to have some drinks
Bouncer: Take a look at the sign
then tell me what you think about . . .

Trick-Knee Trixie
She goes backwards and forwards
No one knows the way
Trick-Knee Trixie will sway

Narrator: Afterwards . . .
Husband: What a show! We gotta go
again and again and again!
Wife: You can go, that's a show that's only fun for men

(from *HENWAY - Big Hair*)

Truth Decay

Your lines are thin
You're spread too thin
I would begin to wonder why

Palms are sweaty
Body's sweaty
Are you ready to tell a lie?

Brush your wisdom teeth more often,
your breath smells of truth decay
Keep lying through those yellow teeth,
the overbite will stay

Must it happen?
I must be happening to me right now
Friends are here
I have no fear you'll be all over town

Brush your wisdom teeth more often,
your breath smells of truth decay
Keep trying to get off cheap,
the end is when you'll pay

More attention
Good intentions
Prevention leads to cure
If your name remains on someone's plaque
they'll brush you off for sure

Brush your wisdom teeth more often,
your breath smells of truth decay
Psychosis leads to halitosis
Both must go away
today

(unrecorded)

Try This On For Size

How about a hat made of calico cat?
So soft and furry
It's alive, don't worry
Here's a sweater knit from Swiss chocolate
It's too warm for summer,
and melting's a bummer

You think these clothes are weird,
but there is no need to be scared
You gotta trust me when I say . . .

Try this on for size
Won't believe your eyes
Fits you like a glove
We are talking love it!

Take a look at that shoe of blue kangaroo
Hopping through the air
beats shopping for footwear
Snap on one of these cucumberbunds
Green looks incredible,
plus this tux is edible

You think I flipped my lid
but I've got news for you kid
For sure, odd is in today

Try this on for size
Won't believe your eyes
Fits you like a glove
We are talking love it!

Clothes make the man,
especially when the dude is see-through
So why not look grand
'cause you never know who'll you'll bump into?

Try this on for size
Won't believe your eyes
Fits you like a glove
We are talking love it!

(from *Purple Burt*)

What a Gas!

Hello there Burt, hello there Kurt
Won't you please tuck in your shirts?
As you can see, there are many things
that can spill or simply spurt

Allow me please to introduce
my humble self to both of youse
My name is Doctor Fritz von Nozzle
The gas I make I store in bozzles

I understand you that you have come
to fill your jars with perhaps some
of my new mixtures and concoctions?
To transfer them we will need suction

A spritz of this, a squirt of those
A swizzle stick goes to and frose
Then over heat, I bring my beaker
Tiptoe up and take a peeker

What a gas I have in here!
What a gas! Yes it is clear
What a gas! I so love mixing!
What's the gas I have been fixing?

I've made some hydrogen and lowdrogen
Some speedium and slowdrogen
Loop-d'loopogen and poop-poop-d'doopogen
Some sillium, some serious
Boron and curious
Half an itty bitty liter of some peterpumpkinether
Propane and amateuric
mixed with trick neon from Zurich
Funny thing, it makes me laugh
I've used all my laughing gas!

So step right up and pop your stoppers
I'll fill your jars to the toppers!

What a gas you'll have with these!
What, a gas? No they won't freeze
What a gas! Enjoy my gasses!
Now can you help me find my glasses?

(from *Purple Burt*)

What Goes Around Comes Around

When I was a little kid
I could not tell right from wrong
Never questioned what I did
Even brought my friends along

What goes around comes around

As a teen things headed south
Like a fool I fought the law
Got kicked from school for my mouth
They're gonna learn that this is war

What goes around comes around

I will take what's rightly mine
even if you think it's yours
To be denied would be a crime
I play the game to settle scores

What goes around comes around
goes around comes around
goes around comes around

I am bad at being good
I am good at being bad

If you think I can be tamed
you had better think again
You're the one that will be blamed
when we reach the bitter end

What goes around comes around
goes around comes around
goes around comes around

(rough demo)

When I Was Your Age

When I was your age in double zero
everyone lived on the planet Earth
I had a lover,
house in the suburbs,
worked a lot and always said "Hello"

But now it's 2099
Oh how those old days look divine
So sonny would you be so kind
and help me into some new brine?

Sure we may not be able to see anymore
but you know we've still got nostalgia

At double zero there was a fear of
everything shutting down for good
But nothing happened
except some laughing
Auld Lang Syne, confetti and balloons

And life continued as it was
People were happy just because
Too bad they couldn't hear the buzz
of future visitors from Zuzzz

Sure we may not be able to breathe anymore
but you know we've still got nostalgia

They came in 2024
Apparently they turned the shore
into an incinerator
Good thing we moved to Mars before
they melted bombs and guns and planes
and made robots from the remains
so peace could always be maintained
Oh yeah, they also took our brains

For forty years the Earth was theirs
but human beings had no cares
Happiness happened everywhere
until the '64 World's Fair

When I was your age people had babies
they would raise up into an adult
It wasn't easy
with all the sleazies
and the temptation to go astray

But now in 2099
offspring are springing up just fine
125 and I'm ready to give birth one more time

Sure we may not be able to see anymore
but you know we've still got nostalgia
Sure we may not be able to breathe anymore
but you know we've still got nostalgia
Sure we may not be able to grieve anymore
but you know we've still got nostalgia
Sure we may not be able to leave anymore
but you know we've still got nostalgia

(from *FRED*)

When Your Number's Up

When your number's up
You jump on the dance floor, ready to rock

When your number's up
The lottery jackpot check is on the way

When your number's up
Telemarketers just won't take no for an answer

When your number's up
You no longer need *Frazier* as a lead-in

When your number's up
Shake the thermometer, then climb back in bed

When your number's up
Sold! To the man with the turquoise necktie

When your number's up
Advance three spaces and roll again

When your number's up
Larry King says "Brooklyn, New York, you're on the air"

When your number's up
The proud new papa presses his face against the glass

When your number's up
You start to think that maybe Jared's on to something

When your number's up
All that studying doesn't seem like such a bummer

When your number's up
Put down the *People*, the doctor will see you now

When your number's up
The maitre d' will show you to your table

When your number's up
Blow out those candles on your cake

When your number's up
The dealer slides a pile of chips in your direction

When your number's up
Pick out the cheesecake you've had your eyes on

When your number's up
NASDAQ is the sweetest sound you've ever heard

When your number's up
You're dead

(unreleased)

Where'd Ya Get That Dirt?

All the day we lay around in bed
Just a bunch of full-time sleepyheads
As hard as we try to open up our eyes
it's so much easier to yawn and take a nap instead

If only there was something we could use
to help us undo our daily snooze
There's a kid we know who's always on the go
He's eatin' soil, maybe that boy'll share,
let's ask him
Yo . . .

Where'd ya get that dirt? (Hey Purple Burt)
Where'd ya get that dirt? (What dirt? That dirt)
Where'd ya get that dirt?
Where'd ya get that dirt?

Burt . . .
You stay alert by eating dirt
It's on your shirt
We see it
So be a bud, show us the mud
Can't you afford a wee bit?

One day one of us will stay awake
to track down the sound that shovel makes
'Cause while we're asleep someone's digging deep
If there's enough of that special stuff
please help out your peeps

Where'd ya get that dirt? (Hey Purple Burt)
Where'd ya get that dirt? (What dirt? That dirt)
Where'd ya get that dirt?
Where'd ya get that dirt?

(from *Purple Burt*)

Who May I Say Is Calling?

You're funny, you're dour
You're sweet and you're sour
You're grungy, you're stunning
You're stoic, you're punning

You're honest, corrupt
Relaxed yet abrupt
You're giggling, you're bawling
Who may I say is calling?

You're winsome, you're crabby
You're quiet yet gabby
You're supple, you're brittle
Sure yet noncommittal

You're secure, you're needy
You're veggie, you're meaty
You're minute, you're sprawling
Who may I say is calling?

You're someone, no one
and everyone at once
You're one of the Funts,
and I am your dunce

You're bubbly, you're bleak
You're stubbly, you're chic
You're trusty, you're shifty
You're wasteful yet thrifty

You're wingnut, you're lib
You're blatant, you're glib
You're prompt yet you're stalling
Who may I say is calling?

You're subtle, you're pointed
Stiff yet double-jointed

Convenient but distant
Erratic, consistent

You're morose, you're chipper
You're devout, you're stripper
Upstanding, yet falling
Who may I say is calling?

(unrecorded)

Wonder Where

I wonder where my underwear is,
wonder where?
I wonder where my underwear is,
wonder where?
I wonder where my underwear is?
Wonder where what's under there is?
I wonder where my underwear is,
wonder where?

I wonder how my bouncing cow is,
wonder how?
I wonder how my bouncing cow is,
wonder how?
When I ask him if his feet ache
all that comes out is a milkshake
I wonder how my bouncing cow is,
wonder how?

I wonder who invented blue,
I wonder who?
I wonder who invented blue,
I wonder who?
Did he spill red on the blue
and then invent some purple too?
I wonder who invented blue,
I wonder who?

It's great to ask questions about everything
But it's even more fun to do it while you're singing

I wonder why I cannot fly,
I wonder why?
I wonder why I cannot fly,
I wonder why?
Feather me and give a small push
You will hear "flap flap flap" then "Smush!"

I wonder why I cannot fly,
I wonder why?

I wonder if a fish can sniff,
I wonder if?
I wonder if a fish can sniff,
I wonder if?
'Cause if a fish can sniff through water
could it smell the guy that caught her?
I wonder if a fish can sniff,
I wonder if?

I wonder when this song will end,
I wonder when?
I wonder when this song will end,
I wonder when?
I wonder when this song will end,
I wonder when?
I wonder when this song will end,
I wonder when?

(from *Purple Burt*)

About the Author

Mitch Friedman is a one-man band from Brooklyn, New York. His concept album for kids, *Purple Burt*, won the 2005 National Parenting Publications (NAPPA) Honors Award. He has collaborated with long-time friends Andy Partridge and Dave Gregory of XTC, and home recording pioneer R. Stevie Moore. In 1998, he attended a one-week long songwriting course in England, taught by Ray Davies of The Kinks.

His non-musical pursuits have included ironic street photography, improv/sketch comedy/monologue writing and performance, and film/video editing. He is also the author of the tragicomic memoir *Hell Toupee*.

www.mitchfriedman.com
www.purpleburt.com
www.gameshowteeth.com
www.mitchfriedman.com/SING-SING
my.bookbaby.com/book/hell-toupee

www.ingramcontent.com/pod-product-compliance
Lightning Source LLC
Chambersburg PA
CBHW061324040426
42444CB00011B/2758